give your gifts

the prayer services

G-4946
$24.95

give your gifts

the prayer services

Other resources in this series:

G-4946FS Give Your Gifts: Full Score and Teaching CD
G-4946A Give Your Gifts: Choir Edition
CD/CS-452 Give Your Gifts: The Basics
CD/CS-454 Give Your Gifts: The Songs

Linda M. Baltikas

Robert W. Piercy

with a foreword by Jean E. Bross-Judge

GIA Publications, Inc.
Chicago

Cover art: Katherine Dunn, Minneapolis, Minnesota
Cover design: The Kantor Group, Inc., Minneapolis, Minnesota
Book design and layout: Robert M. Sacha
Editor: Neil Borgstrom

Give Your Gifts:
The Prayer Services
ISBN: 1-57999-059-2
Copyright © 1999
GIA Publications, Inc.
7404 S. Mason Ave. Chicago, IL 60638
1.800.GIA.1358 or 708.496.3800 • www.giamusic.com

TABLE OF CONTENTS

Foreword by Jean E. Bross-Judge vii
Acknowledgments ix
Introduction x

Eucharistic Celebration for High School Staff Retreat 1
    Order of Worship 3
    Catechist/teacher information page 7

Eucharistic Celebration of the New School Year 8
    Order of Worship 10
    Catechist/teacher information page 16

Morning Prayer 17
    Order of Worship 19
    Catechist/teacher information page 23

Prayer Service of Justice for Teams and Ensembles 24
    Order of Worship 26
    Catechist/teacher information page 29

Eucharistic Celebration of Class Unity 30
    Order of Worship 32
    Catechist/teacher information page 37

Eucharistic Commissioning Service of School/Group Leadership 38
    Order of Worship 40
    Catechist/teacher information page 45

Commissioning Service for Community Service 46
    Order of Worship 48
    Catechist/teacher information page 51

Evening Prayer for Evening Meeting 52
    Order of Worship 54
    Catechist/teacher information page 56

Eucharistic Celebration of the Feast of All Saints 57
    Order of Worship 59
    Catechist/teacher information page 63

Eucharistic Celebration in the Face of Death 64
    Order of Worship 67
    Catechist/teacher information page 71

Eucharistic Celebration of Thanksgiving 72
    Order of Worship 74
    Catechist/teacher information page 78

Advent Reconciliation Service 79
    Order of Worship 82
    Catechist/teacher information page 85

Eucharistic Celebration in Honor of the Blessed Virgin Mary 86
    Order of Worship 88
    Catechist/teacher information page 91

Prayer Service to Bless the New Year 92
    Order of Worship 94
    Catechist/teacher information page 98

Eucharistic Celebration of Martin Luther King Day
(or in celebration of Black History Month) 99
    Order of Worship 101
    Catechist/teacher information page 105

Ash Wednesday Prayer Service 106
    Order of Worship 108
    Catechist/teacher information page 111

Lenten Reconciliation Service 112
    Order of Worship 114
    Catechist/teacher information page 117

Eucharistic Celebration of the Ascension 118
    Order of Worship 120
    Catechist/teacher information page 123

Eucharistic Baccalaureate 124
    Order of Worship 126
    Catechist/teacher information page 131

Eucharistic Celebration of the End of the School Year 132
    Order of Worship 134
    Catechist/teacher information page 138

Appendix 139
Glossary 141
Bibliography 143
About the Authors 144

FOREWORD

As a liturgical music ensemble director, I once worked with a group of high school young women to prepare for a December 8 "Immaculate Conception" school liturgy. Several members of the high school's chorus asked to sing the arrangement of "Hail, Holy Queen Enthroned Above" made popular by the hit movie *Sister Act*. Their reasons were compelling: the text fit the feast, it was a tune from the traditional repertoire of the church, and the arrangement was "current" and "singable." They were convinced that their peers would "get into it!" Their liturgical, musical, and pastoral judgments seemed to come right out of *Music and Catholic Worship*.

At the conclusion of the liturgy, during which participation from the all-female student body was moderate (at best), the choir approached the microphones. Their angelic voices raised the traditional hymn, commanding the participation, nostalgic smiles, and approval of numerous faculty members. Then, without missing a beat, they broke into an up-tempo arrangement of the hymn. Just as predicted, their peers "got into it" and began clapping and singing along with them.

It was at that moment that I noticed a handful of faculty members who, just moments before were fully participating in the music, were now headed for the exit doors, their heads shaking in disgust and mouths murmuring words like "disrespectful," "sacrilegious," and "no boundaries." The song, in my estimation, remained a sound choice for that liturgy with that group of youth *and* adults who gathered for that celebration.

Paragraph 14 from the *Constitution on the Sacred Liturgy* states: "The Church earnestly desires that all the faithful be led to that full, conscious, and active participation in liturgical celebrations called for by the very nature of the liturgy." In recent years, youth ministers, liturgists, musicians, and young people have engaged in dialog to wrestle with the promotion of active participation of youth in liturgy. As a participant in many dialogs, I have heard a strong voice that often declares that "we (adults) must teach them (youth) how to participate." I believe that we must present them with the traditional prayer of our Church, but then we must be able to learn from them how they can best express prayer within those traditional guidelines.

In the spring of 1999, I watched news coverage of the funerals and prayer services for the shooting victims from Columbine High School in Littleton, Colorado. I was keenly aware of the roles of youth and adults in those worship settings. Young people were expressing their memories and grief *within* a variety of traditions through song writing, creating memorials, compiling videos, writing on caskets, and speaking words of truth about their deceased peers. Those young people knew a lot about how they needed to ritualize and pray about that horrific tragedy. And the adults? They knew how to provide the comfort of religious tradition, how to incorporate contemporary cultural expressions, how to gently shepherd young people through the experience, and how to engage in prayer alongside young people.

"Greater youth participation in the liturgy will not occur without an intentional effort to seek and encourage it. Parents, pastors, parish priests, youth and youth leaders, liturgy committees, and concerned individuals need to create a local pastoral plan. . . . We need to intentionally invite them to participate in our ongoing mission." (Paragraph 12, *From Age to Age: The Challenge of Worship with Adolescents*, The National Federation for Catholic Youth Ministry, Inc., 1997.)

Give Your Gifts is an excellent resource for those who desire to *intentionally* embrace the challenge of worship with adolescents. Whether you are working in a parish, school, or retreat center setting, the prayer services and rituals can serve as a launch pad as you create your pastoral plan. Some of the music and prayer forms might be familiar to you while others might be new. Remember that *Give Your Gifts* is a resource that is meant to be adapted to serve your group. The accompanying recording features songs that were recorded by a group of high school students. As one who witnessed the recording process, I assure you that the diversity of music represented is a reflection of the diverse musical and spiritual tastes of those young people. I have yet to encounter one of those young recording artists who doesn't skip at least one song while listening to the recording!

The Church's prayer traditions are well represented in *Give Your Gifts*. Your challenge is to gather young people, engage them in the preparation process, and encourage their expression and participation. Perhaps your greater task is to remain patient and faithful to the process, which will undoubtedly occur in God's time!

—Jean E. Bross-Judge

ACKNOWLEDGMENTS

All working on the project want to thank Alec Harris, vice-president of GIA Publications, and the entire senior staff for their belief in a very daunting process. Michael Cymbala needs special attention for bringing Baltikas and Piercy together and also for challenging all of us to "remember the audience—the teens themselves." Neil Borgstrom receives a special nod for editing this manuscript. Aside from the fast pace, changes daily in authors' ideas, musician suggestions, and never knowing where Piercy was in the United States, Neil persevered and we all appreciate the hard work. Neil contributed (along with Bob Sacha) in making a book that is not only helpful but also quite well thought through on layout.

GIVE YOUR GIFTS

First things first. *Give Your Gifts* is an effort to provide sound liturgies for the young people of our Catholic faith. So often we think that they can't pray, don't want to pray, or simply are bored with religion because so much is going on in their lives. Yes, the aforementioned may be true, but it has been found that there is a spiritual hunger in our young people, and we are all called to meet them in their world. We are challenged to understand their story and to allow them to "give their gifts" while adults also "give *their* gifts"!

This book was developed over an eighteen-month process. Author Linda Baltikas is well respected in the Chicago area for her sense of liturgy and her work at Queen of Peace High School in Burbank, Illinois. Robert Piercy, nationally known as a liturgy speaker, comes with a knowledge of a study done of youth around this country. It was the hope of GIA Publications to provide a comprehensive resource for celebrating liturgy with young people. (Notice no age is given, since the term *young people* can mean many things depending on the area of the United States.)

This book has a direct correlation to the CDs, cassettes, and music scores also called *Give Your Gifts*. The project recordings were produced by Gary Daigle (another realist in the music of youth culture) and directed by Kate Cuddy (1999 Teacher of the Year for her work in musical direction in Minnesota). It was Kate's choir from Benilde–St. Margaret's High School in St. Louis Park, Minnesota, that recorded the music. During the first recording sessions of the summer of 1998, we all knew we had something unique, because we finally had youth ministering to and for youth, all walking toward the new millennium.

In no way are these liturgies to be considered the only way to pray or the music the only choices or styles. This book is a *workbook* for those who prepare liturgy. Although much material is given here, each person needs to look at his or her own situation and make suitable adaptations. When this project was first envisioned, the book was to be only for Catholic high school settings, and yet, as we began to study the youth culture around the country, we found that many youth ministries or high school catechetical programs also celebrate the same events. We considered these situations in the notes, but we want to encourage anyone using this book to feel free to change text to fit a parish setting where students from many high schools come and celebrate.

So what is in this book? Let's go through what you will find for each liturgy. Before an actual liturgy you will find preparation pages. These begin with **GETTING STARTED**. Here you will find some overall thoughts to jump-start your own ideas. Specific information is given on choice of Scripture or background on where the authors are coming from regarding this liturgy.

In the **MINISTERS** section you will find a listing of ministers you will need. Items of special attention you may want to pass onto various ministers and assistants are also given.

So often we must create the prayer space. Liturgy is celebrated in a gym or relegated to the "extra" room in the parish building. The ENVIRONMENT section becomes a resource to find helpful ideas to make the worship space come alive specific to this liturgy. It is assumed a school or religious education program has access to such items as the ritual books, candles (including paschal candle), cross, incense, sacred vessels, and the appropriate liturgical garb for various ministers.

The MUSIC section coordinates with the recordings and music books. Practical pastoral music notes are given here. This section is intended to give pause to all the planners so that music is not just "added on" but becomes an integral part of the prayer.

LITURGY CHECKLIST is rather self-explanatory and has been found to be quite helpful. Right before a liturgy many things are happening, but here is space where you can keep organized by checking tasks and items off. There is ample white space given so you can add other things needed in your situation. Use pencil here so that you can erase after the liturgy and use the list again next year.

The wide margins on all these pages are intended for you to make notes and even mark down your thoughts from year to year.

The **ORDER OF WORSHIP** contains the texts for the actual liturgy. It is easy to find by the black box found in the upper corner of each page. Music again corresponds in number to the recordings and music book of *Give Your Gifts*. (Please note that there are two different recordings. One is called *Give Your Gifts: The Songs* and the other is called *Give Your Gifts: The Basics*.)

For the ritual prayers we have provided two options. The first option is to use the Sacramentary (or other ritual book indicated). In references to the Sacramentary, the first number indicates where the prayer can be found in the edition published by Catholic Book Publishing. The number in parentheses is the same prayer but corresponds to the page number of the edition published by Liturgical Press. The printed prayer, the second option, is an alternative prayer written in a language faithful to the Scripture and ritual but also sensitive to the youth culture.

HOMILY/REFLECTION NOTES are just that: questions to ignite an idea in preparing to share the Scripture message with youth. *They are not to be used as questions to ask the assembly!* Instead, the presider, homilist, or Scripture sharer may want to keep a journal of these questions as a means of gathering ideas before a final homily is prepared. These questions would also be appropriate if you are gathering with students to share in a homily preparation session with the presider.

Any ritual described here needs to be thought through for your own community. These have all been tested in some format, yet it was found that each community trying these out still had uniqueness. A word of caution for any liturgy coordinator: Think, even walk, through the ritual very carefully before you actually do this at liturgy. A well-intended ritual can fall flat if there is confusion on who is supposed to stand where or say what!

A unique feature to this book is the reproducible page found at the end of the liturgy. The purchaser of this book is granted permission to make as many copies of this page as needed. Before copying, the liturgy coordinator or campus minister needs to fill in Date, Time, Location, any changes in the readings from Scripture, and name of the contact person. The other material on the page is very helpful for faculty, catechists, youth ministers, and staff members. Copies could be placed in their mailboxes or lesson plans prior to a service. It is always good to go over the readings with the assembly prior to the liturgy. If possible, make this part of catechetical sessions, religion classes, theology modules, or even homeroom. The actual Questions for Students to Ponder may be used as preparation—or better yet, mystagogy after liturgy. Have students keep a liturgical journal where these questions may be copied and they can journal their experience throughout the year.

In closing, use your gifts to the best of your ability. Liturgical renewal will not happen overnight, but we can all make a change by welcoming our young people into the vision that liturgy is a metaphor for life. (Thank you, John Gallen, for that image.) As you use this book and have stories to share or suggestions, please contact us at GIA. We are always interested in knowing your thoughts, ideas, and suggestions (contact us at www.giamusic.com). Now is the moment for us to move forward with the identity of our faith that comes through ritual!

EUCHARISTIC CELEBRATION FOR HIGH SCHOOL STAFF RETREAT
AUGUST / BEGINNING OF THE ACADEMIC YEAR

PREPARATION

GETTING STARTED

Though most high schools and parishes have a retreat program in place for the students, the same energy may not be invested in securing a retreat day for the staff. Teachers and service personnel are inundated with in-service training, meetings, workshops, and daily activities so they may have to be convinced that a retreat is not the same thing. A day of retreat provides the staff with the chance to "retreat" from all the busyness of the day-to-day life of the school and come away to rest awhile to refresh and renew the spirit. An integral part of the day should be prayer together as an adult faith community. The readings chosen focus on taking some time away from the usual. The first reading from Kings is the story of Ezekiel, who goes off to look for the Lord. When Ezekiel fails to find the Lord in the usual places, he experiences the Lord in a way he never expected. In Matthew, we hear those comforting words of Jesus, who invites those of us who are burdened and need rest to come to him. Just as with the adolescents they teach and serve, the staff of the school represent different levels of faith development. It would not be realistic to think that one retreat day and one liturgy could meet everyone's spiritual needs, but just setting aside this one day without notes to take or a project to complete should have universal appeal. Depending on the time of year that this liturgy takes place, some symbol or reminder of the renewal might be given to the members of the staff at this Mass.

MINISTERS

The staff members themselves should be invited to take the roles of lector, intercessor, and eucharistic ministers. The reader should be asked early in the day and be given a copy of the reading to review before the liturgy. Since the campus minister would know most of the staff, he or she would approach those who are comfortable reading at Mass. It would also be presumed that there are members of the staff who are mandated to distribute Communion. Depending on the size of the assembly, only one or two additional ministers would be needed. Ideally, the celebrant has been involved in the retreat day, but if that is not feasible, some time should be spent with him regarding the day's focus.

ENVIRONMENT

Depending on the size of the assembly and the space used for the liturgy, an entrance procession with cross and candles may be awkward. The cross and candles should already be in place. The water and aspergill for the sprinkling rite should also be near the altar and accessible for the celebrant. There should be an ambo with the Lectionary already in position. To further enhance the worship space, any additional use of color, flowers, etc. should be appropriate to the season.

MUSIC

The music selections for this liturgy are songs that can be picked up immediately—in fact, they may not even require a worship aid. If you are using music selections other than those suggested, be sure they are well known by the community. Remember, the first time praying together should celebrate diversity, not cause division. As with all the liturgies from this book, make sure that the music comes alive. Even if the community has sung a song for years, consider a new obbligato or rhythm pattern to make it fresh.

Although this is a faculty/catechists and staff retreat, the music director may have already been in contact with some students to train as cantors. Use them. Let them lead, and have them challenge the staff that sung liturgy will be a celebration of unity!

LITURGY CHECKLIST

❑ Copies of readings, given to readers in advance
❑ Copy of intercessions, given to intercessor in advance
❑ Vestments for presider
❑ Lectionary, marked and in place
❑ Sacramentary, marked and in place
❑ Water and aspergill for sprinkling
❑ Bread, wine, water, ciboria and communion cups, corporal, purificator(s), finger bowl, finger towel
❑ Processional cross in place
❑ Incense pot, incense resins (in incense boat?), charcoal (lit)
❑ Candles in place and lit
❑ Worship aids distributed
Other:

ORDER OF WORSHIP

INTRODUCTORY RITES

GATHERING SONG

"He Came Down / We Are Marching (Siyahumba)," basics CD/CS1-#2, music book #15.

GREETING

After the greeting the presider may wish to included these or similar words of introduction:

Today, the adult members of this faith community
have come away to renew themselves
and seek the Lord in unexpected places.

Come to the water,
be refreshed,
and bless each other.

SPRINKLING RITE

Reprise "We Are Marching" during sprinkling rite.

May almighty God cleanse us of our sins, . . .

GLORIA

"Glory to God," basics CD/CS1-#3, music book #16. *Music may continue through opening prayer into the reprise.*

OPENING PRAYER
Or: *Sacramentary*, p. 898
(812), #16, For Pastoral
or Spiritual Meetings

Let us pray.

God our creator,
we know that you are with us always
and you wait patiently
for us to spend time in your presence;
yet, our lives get so busy,
we often cannot find time to quiet ourselves
and hear your voice.
Make us aware of the need for you in our lives
so that we may often come to you
when we are burdened and need rest.

We ask this through our Lord Jesus Christ,
who lives and reigns with you and the Holy Spirit,
one God, for ever and ever. R/.

Reprise "We Are Marching."

LITURGY OF THE WORD

READING 1

1 Kings 19:4–9, 11–15, Lectionary #784-3
Always observe some silence after the reading.

PSALM

"Psalm 135: We Praise You," basics CD/CS1-#8, music book #21.
Observe some silence after the psalm.

GOSPEL ACCLAMATION

"Word of Truth and Life," basic CD/CS2-#6, music book #31.
You may wish to incense the gospel. See the appendix for suggestions.

GOSPEL

Matthew 11:25–30, Lectionary #742-3

**HOMILY/
REFLECTION NOTES**

You may want to consider the following questions as you prepare your homily.
When have you found God in unexpected places?
Where are some of the unexpected places in which you have experienced
   God's presence?
What are some difficulties you have in taking some time away to renew
   yourself?
Where has your own search for God taken you?
What can you do this year in your ministry of teaching that would allow God
   to reveal himself to you in the students?

**GENERAL
INTERCESSIONS**

Or: "Prayer of the Faithful," basics CD/CS2-#10, music book #35.
*Be sure to add any intentions that are pertinent to your community. The intercessor
should be in place before the presider gives the invitation to pray. These prayers may
be led from the ambo.*

Presider:

**God of comfort and rest,
you know us better than we know ourselves.
Listen to our prayers as we bring them before you.**

*Musicians begin mantra of "Come and Fill Our Hearts," basics CD/CS2-#9,
music book #34. Sing three times before intercessor begins to pray the intercessions.
During the spoken intercessions continue with instrumental accompaniment under-
neath.*

Intercessor:

**We pray for all those who minister to others in retreat work: give
them the Spirit of Wisdom, Counsel, and Right Judgment as they
guide others.**

**We pray for those who are restless, searching, and uncertain of their
way: may they find rest and peace in you**

**We pray for each of us here who educate and guide young people:
may our spirits be renewed.**

**We pray for those who have mentored, listened to, and guided us: that
they be blessed for their patient and generous hearts.**

Are there other things for which we petition God? . . .

For those who have died, especially _____: may they rest in the peace of Christ.

Sing mantra two more times.

The intercessor should face the presider and not leave until the prayer is finished.

Presider: **Loving God,**
we are confident that you have heard our prayers
and we trust in your goodness.
We ask all of this in the name of Jesus, your Son. R/.

Continue to sing mantra throughout the preparation of the gifts.

LITURGY OF THE EUCHARIST

PREPARATION OF THE ALTAR AND THE GIFTS

PRAYER OVER THE GIFTS
Or: *Sacramentary,*
p. 898 *(812)*, #16,
For Pastoral or
Spiritual Meetings

Almighty God and loving Father,
accept these gifts that we offer as a sign of our love.
Help us to understand the importance
of prayer and renewal in our lives.

We ask this in the name of Jesus, your Son. R/.

EUCHARISTIC PRAYER
Sacramentary, p. 556 *(517)*, Eucharistic Prayer IV
Eucharistic Acclamations, basics CD/CS2-#11, music book #36.

COMMUNION RITE

LORD'S PRAYER

SIGN OF PEACE

BREAKING OF THE BREAD
"Lamb of God," basics CD/CS2-#12, music book #37.
Ask the other ministers to help break bread and pour wine so this rite will not be extended.

COMMUNION SONG
"For Living, for Dying," songs CD/CS-#5, music book #5.
Always observe some silence after Communion.

5

PRAYER AFTER COMMUNION

Or: *Sacramentary*, p. 898 (812), #16, For Pastoral or Spiritual Meetings

Let us pray.

God of all life,
may the Holy Communion we have shared
renew and unite us in the important work
of spreading the Gospel.
Give us strength and hope to continue
to be effective ministers of education.

We ask this in the name of Jesus, your Son. R/.

CONCLUDING RITE

GREETING AND BLESSING

Or: *Sacramentary*, p. 575 (533), #13, Ordinary Time IV

Call the staff forward; if the group is not large, call each person by name.
Begin music: "Blessing," basics CD/CS2-#16, music book #41.

Bow your heads and pray for God's blessing.

May God bless you and your educational ministry in this community,
especially as you live out the Gospel message to serve others. R/.

May Christ bless you in your actions
that will form the faith and Catholic identity
of our students. R/.

May the Holy Spirit ignite a fire in your soul
allowing our young people
to see your commitment to education. R/.

Sing blessing twice.

And may almighty God bless you (us) and your (our) work,
the Father, and the Son, ✠ and the Holy Spirit. R/.

DISMISSAL

Begin percussion sounds.

Our celebration has ended.
Let us march, dance, and sing
as we go forward to love and serve the Lord. R/.

RECESSIONAL SONG

"We Are Marching," basics CD/CS1-#2, music book #15.

PREPARATION FOR EUCHARISTIC CELEBRATION FOR HIGH SCHOOL STAFF RETREAT

GIVE THE GIFT OF PERSONAL MINISTRY

DATE: **TIME:**

LOCATION:

OVERALL THEME   We are called to ministry. It is Christ's invitation and we respond. Although our task is burdensome at times, we are called to depend on the risen Christ as our hope and strength.

SCRIPTURE USED   1 Kings 19:4–9, 11–15 / Matthew 11:25–30

SHORT REFLECTION   Throughout the year you will receive these sheets to use with your homeroom or religious education class to prepare for or reflect on the liturgies with the students. It would be very helpful if you began your own journal, using Scripture readings and Questions to Ponder as a way to challenge yourself to move from educator/catechist to co-journeyer with students when at liturgy. Let the liturgies this year be a time for your own spiritual growth. You may also want to use the Questions to Ponder as ways to begin faculty/catechists meetings.

QUESTIONS FOR STAFF TO PONDER
1. What are your hopes and dreams for this year?
2. How have you experienced God over the past summer?
3. What obstacles prevent you from seeing God in all things?
4. How can you find balance between your ministry and your life outside of the classroom?
5. What gift of yours can you share with your students?

CLOSING COMMENTS   You may want to copy your thoughts and put the questions and answers and Scripture citations in a place or places where you will see them throughout your day. May you always remember you are blessing!

Any questions, please contact _____.

EUCHARISTIC CELEBRATION
OF THE NEW SCHOOL YEAR
SEPTEMBER

PREPARATION

GETTING STARTED

The beginning of the school year is much like a brand new year for young people in high school—their lives are on an August-to-June cycle during these four years, and this time of year is not unlike beginning the civil year on January 1. For many, realistically, the return to school brings them back to their only faith community. Here, then, is an opportunity to tap into the energy and enthusiasm that accompanies the start of a new school year by making this first experience of Eucharist a welcoming one. Calling attention to the newest members of the student community—especially the first-year students (freshmen)—and new staff members will heighten the sense of community and belonging. Because it is a new year, returning students and staff also recognize that they have a chance to start over again, whether it is improving academically, building new relationships, or strengthening existing friendships. It is a time for goal setting, making resolutions, and beginning again—all in the context of the school as a praying and worshiping community. As a part of this liturgy, each level in the community is invited to make a commitment or resolution for this school year.

As a way to acknowledge the uniqueness of each class, perhaps the officers of each of the four groups could be invited to create a banner to be carried in at the entrance procession, used as part of the environment during this liturgy, and utilized as a symbol of the class or group at a variety of gatherings—liturgies, retreats, etc.

Because it is the first time the whole community is gathering for prayer, it might be necessary to practice some of the music and responses as well as restate procedures for receiving Communion. This should all take place before the liturgy begins, not during the service.

MINISTERS

Because this is so early in the academic year, ministry teams/groups might not be in place as yet. Those responsible for planning the liturgy may want to look to the older members of the community to serve as lectors and to lead the intercessions. It is important, however, that students assume these roles in the liturgy rather than teachers or other adults. There are certain to be some juniors or seniors who have had experience in proclaiming the Word and leading prayer. The same applies to music ministers.

If the presider is a member of the community, it would be appropriate to invite him to preach; however, if he is not, some other person who is more familiar with the life of the school or parish community would be the better choice because she or he would be in a position to make connections with the Scripture and the lives of the young people in this particular setting. If the principal, campus minister, or youth minister is comfortable in this role, she or he should be looked to, especially in setting the tone for starting the new school year.

Depending on the size of the assembly, eucharistic ministers will be needed. If students have been mandated to serve in this capacity, review of procedures and practice will be necessary.

ENVIRONMENT

If the liturgy is held in a gym or auditorium, preparing the environment is necessary to help transform the space as much as possible. Depending on the size of the space, green plants will help focus attention on the altar and the ambo. If there is a budget, the purchase of flowers with autumn colors will further enhance the worship space. Think of creating banner poles that could use school colors but no words. Fill the space with candles in hurricane lamps or use votive candles. If the liturgy will be celebrated in a gym or multipurpose space, don't fight the space; instead, use less things but in larger proportions (e.g., consider a large cross—something two people could carry in). Don't forget doorways or other areas where you can use candles, plants, icons on small side tables, or combinations of these. Don't decorate just the altar area; infuse the entire room. If special banners have been created for this Mass, stands also need to be in place.

MUSIC

It is a new school year and we gather together to "give our gifts." Make this liturgy move; make it music from the soul. Don't be inhibited by lack of singing—take the assembly's breath away! At the very least, get a few students together and help them to help you "make the change." Do consider using the same set of sung eucharistic acclamations throughout the year; obtain "variety" here by changing their accompaniment. For this first gathering, however, make the eucharistic acclamations truly soulful in sound; don't let down. The penitential rite flows out of the opening "rap" piece, "Now." It has to have soul. The recorded version uses adults and teens together. For the opening procession here, just use the refrain. The suggested communion song is often thought of as a "gathering song," but it's repetition allows young people to "gather" at the table. Using the arrangement on the recording, one has to move and worship God.

LITURGY CHECKLIST

- ❑ Copies of readings, given to readers in advance
- ❑ Copy of intercessions, given to intercessor in advance
- ❑ Vestments for presider
- ❑ Lectionary, marked and in place
- ❑ Sacramentary, marked and in place
- ❑ Processional cross in place
- ❑ Candles, in place and lit
- ❑ Banners and banner stands in place
- ❑ Bread, wine, water, ciboria and communion cups, corporal, purificator(s), finger bowl, finger towel
- ❑ Worship aids distributed
- ❑ All involved in the procession are in place—lector, intercessor, banner bearers, any assistants, presider

Other:

ORDER OF WORSHIP

INTRODUCTORY RITES

GATHERING SONG

"Now," songs CD/CS-#13, music book #13, refrain only.
Use only the refrain for the procession. Continue with bass and percussion throughout the greeting and into the penitential rite. Listen to the recording as a guide to the penitential rite below.

GREETING

PENITENTIAL RITE
Or: "Now (Penitential rite)," basics CD/CS2-#4, music book #29.
Or: *Sacramentary*, p. 360 *(406)*, invitation B with form C-vi *(c-6)*

My sisters and brothers,
we come together for the first time this year as a community.
We remember our need for forgiveness.

Jesus, you reached out in love to all people:
Lord have mercy. R/.

Jesus, you welcomed each person with kindness and concern:
Christ have mercy. R/.

Jesus, you reminded your friends how important it is to forgive:
Lord have mercy. R/.

May almighty God have mercy on us, forgive us our sins,
and bring us to everlasting life. R/.

OPENING PRAYER
Or: *Sacramentary*, p. 906 *(818)*, #24, Beginning of the Civil Year

Let us pray.

Gentle God,
with each day you give us a new beginning.
We thank you for the rhythm of the seasons
and rejoice in the opportunity to come together in this new
    school year.
Help us to reach out to the stranger
and all who call this community home.

We ask this in the name of Jesus, your Son,
who lives and reigns with you and the Holy Spirit,
one God, for ever and ever. R/.

Repeat refrain, verse 1, refrain of "Now."

LITURGY OF THE WORD

READING 1 Genesis 1:14–18, *Lectionary #841-1*
Always observe some silence after the reading.

PSALM "Psalm 135: We Praise You," basics CD/CS1-#8, music book #21.
Observe some silence after the psalm.

GOSPEL ACCLAMATION "Word of Truth and Life," basics CD/CS2-#6, music book #31.

GOSPEL Matthew 5:13–16, *Lectionary #742-2*

HOMILY/
REFLECTION NOTES
As you prepare the homily, reflect on these questions and ideas:
A new school year is much like the beginning of any new year. What are some
goals and resolutions that surface for you as a new year begins?
What gifts do you consider to be a light that is hidden inside of you that you
can challenge yourself to share this year?
What in creation inspires you to learn more about our world?
Thinking about the freshmen, new teachers, and other new students and staff
members, what makes you feel welcome in a new environment?
When do you feel called to do your best?

RITUAL *After the homily the presider returns to the presidential chair. Begin instrumental
version of "I Say Yes, My Lord," songs CD/CS-#10, music book #10, and continue
to play under the following rite and into the preparation of the gifts.*

Presider: **I invite the Seniors to stand.**
(principal or lead catechist)

**Do you, the Seniors,
continue your commitment to work with all members of the
school community
to ensure that the mission of our school is a lived experience?**

Seniors: **We do.**

Presider: **Do you also realize your responsibilities to exercise leadership
in the creation of a positive atmosphere here at _____?**

Seniors: **We do.**

Presider: **And will you cooperate with the other students,
the faculty, administration, and staff
to bring about leadership in the spirit of Christ's message?**

Seniors: **We will.**

Presider: **In the name of this community,
I accept your commitments
and pray that you be given the strength and courage to work together**

and accept the challenges of the new school year. Amen.

All sing refrain of "I Say Yes, My Lord."

I invite the faculty (catechists), administration, and staff to stand.

Do you, the faculty (catechists), administration, and staff, rededicate yourselves to the service of the young people of_____?

Faculty: We do.

Presider: Do you acknowledge your responsibilities as Christian educators and accept the challenge to live and teach the values of Jesus?

Faculty: We do.

Presider: And do you realize the kind of atmosphere needed in order for all members of this community to achieve their greatest potential, make a commitment, and work together to create a community of justice?

Faculty: We do.

Presider: In the name of this community, I accept your commitments and pray that you be given the strength and courage to work together and accept the challenges of the new school year. Amen.

All sing refrain of "I Say Yes, My Lord."

I invite the Sophomores to stand.

As sophomores, do you accept the challenge to work hard at your studies and to become more involved in making this (school) program a good place to be?

Sophomores: We do.

Presider: And do you ask God to help you live out the values of Jesus?

Sophomores: We do.

Presider: In the name of this community, I accept your commitments and pray that you be given the strength and courage to work together and accept the challenges of the new school year. Amen.

All sing refrain of "I Say Yes, My Lord."

I invite the Juniors to stand.

Do you, the junior class,
accept the challenge to use your talents and abilities in your studies
and also in working together at (school) activities?

Juniors: We do.

Presider: Do you realize
that it is important to look beyond today
and to begin the process of decision making for the future?

Juniors: We do.

And do you ask for the guidance of the Spirit
as you continue to be members of this community
in a more mature, involved way?

Juniors: We do.

Presider: In the name of this community,
I accept your commitments
and pray that you be given the strength and courage to work together
and accept the challenges of the new school year. Amen.

All sing refrain of "I Say Yes, My Lord."

I invite the Freshmen to stand.

Do you, the first-year students and the newest members of the
_____ family,
make a commitment to do your best this year?

Freshmen: We do.

Presider: Do you accept the challenge to grow and mature
as you begin your days as high school students?

Freshmen: We do.

Presider: And do you recognize your responsibilities
to live a Christian life
and follow the invitation of the Gospel to let your light shine?

Freshmen: We do.

Presider: In the name of this community,
I accept your commitments
and pray that you be given the strength and courage to work together
and accept the challenges of the new school year. Amen.

All sing refrain of "I Say Yes, My Lord."

GENERAL
INTERCESSIONS
Or: "Prayer of the Faithful,"
basics CD/CS2-#10,
music book #35.

Make sure to include any intentions unique to your community, especially if there have been deaths or serious illnesses over the summer. The intercessor should be in place before the presider gives the invitation to pray. These prayers may be led from the ambo.

Presider:

**My sisters and brothers,
let us bring our prayers and needs before God.**

Intercessor:

For the leaders of our Church, our nation, our city: that they may teach by example as well as by word, we pray to the Lord: R/.

For our teachers, the principal, and all those who help the young people in this community, we pray to the Lord: R/.

For the students, especially those who are new this year: that they may be given knowledge and courage to live up to their commitments, we pray to the Lord: R/.

For those in our families and among our friends who are sick, especially, _____: that they be given hope, we pray to the Lord: R/.

Other intentions may be added here.

For those who have died, especially _____: that they live in peace forever with you, we pray to the Lord: R/.

The intercessor should face the presider and not leave until the prayer is finished.

Presider:

**God of wisdom,
through Jesus, your Son, you show us the way to live.
Help us to rejoice in new friends and opportunities in this school year.
We ask this through Jesus, the teacher of us all. R/.**

LITURGY OF THE EUCHARIST

PREPARATION OF THE
ALTAR AND THE GIFTS

"I Say Yes, My Lord," songs CD/CS-#10, music book #10, bilingual if possible. Students who are assigned bring forward the gifts of bread, water, and wine.

PRAYER OVER
THE GIFTS
Or: *Sacramentary*, p. 906
(818), #24, Beginning of
the Civil Year

**Loving God,
we bring to you simple gifts of bread and wine;
we offer, too, our hopes and dreams
for this new school year.
Help us to nourish each other with support
as we begin anew.**

We ask this through Jesus Christ, your Son. R/.

EUCHARISTIC PRAYER

Sacramentary, p. 548 (504), Eucharistic Prayer II
"Eucharistic Acclamations," basics CD/CS2-#11, music book #36.

COMMUNION RITE

LORD'S PRAYER

SIGN OF PEACE

BREAKING OF
THE BREAD

"Lamb of God," basics CD/CS2-#12, music book #37.
Ask the other ministers to help break bread and pour wine so this rite will not be extended.

COMMUNION SONG

"Come, All You People," basics CD/CS2-#1, music book #26.
Always observe some silence after Communion.

PRAYER AFTER
COMMUNION
Or: *Sacramentary,* p. 906
*(818), #24, Beginning of
the Civil Year*

Let us pray.

**Creator God,
your Word and the Body and Blood of Jesus nourish us.
May they inspire us to grow as a community of people
who celebrate your presence among us.**

We ask this through Jesus, your Son. R/.

CONCLUDING RITE

GREETING AND
BLESSING
Or: "Blessing," basics
CD/CS2-#16,
music book #41.
Or: *Sacramentary,* p.570
*(529), #3, Beginning of
the New Year*

Bow your heads and pray for God's blessing.

May God bless your minds as you search out new ideas. R/.

**May Christ bless your hands and feet
as you use them in acts of justice. R/.**

**May the Holy Spirit bless your hearts
as you strive to live out the values of faith, hope, and love. R/.**

**May almighty God bless you,
the Father, and the Son, ✠ and the Holy Spirit. R/.**

DISMISSAL

RECESSIONAL SONG

"Now," songs CD/CS-#13, music book #13, *with verses.*

15

PREPARATION FOR EUCHARISTIC CELEBRATION OF THE NEW SCHOOL YEAR

GIVE THE GIFT OF A NEW YEAR

DATE: **TIME:**

LOCATION:

OVERALL THEME	Starting the new academic year by recommitting to the challenges ahead as well as making resolutions with which to achieve goals.
SCRIPTURE USED	Genesis 1:14–18 / Matthew 5:13–16
SHORT REFLECTION	The readings for the opening Mass of the academic year focus on the rhythm of time and seasons as well as the challenges that accompany starting again. Especially in the gospel reading, the students will hear the call to be their best selves in this new year. Rather than grudgingly accept that vacation is over, the young people should be helped to see it in the larger context of creation, valuing each moment as a gift, adopting a "seize the day" mentality, if you will. It would be good to discuss the importance of commitment and challenge as the students embark on the adventure of a new school year.
QUESTIONS FOR STUDENTS TO PONDER	1. What goals or resolutions do you have for this academic year? 2. What help do you need in order to achieve these goals—from teachers, parents, friends? 3. How can you contribute, let your light shine, this year so that this school (group) is more of a community? 4. How can you be more welcoming and inviting, especially to the newest members of the community? 5. What are the clubs and organizations you have considered sharing your time and talents with this year?
CLOSING COMMENTS	If there is a place, the students could be asked to write down a goal or resolution they have for the new school year. These could be displayed in the classroom as a reminder for the year. If the liturgy is to feel like a part of the rhythm of life in the school community, some preparation and follow up is necessary on a regular basis. It is a good idea to start this pattern with the first liturgy of the school year.

Any questions, please contact _____.

MORNING PRAYER

ANYTIME THROUGHOUT THE SCHOOL YEAR

PREPARATION

GETTING STARTED

Morning prayer is the official prayer of the Church for beginning a new day. Because it is intended to be prayed at the break of day, it reminds us of the resurrection of Jesus, the true light. Any variety of events or circumstances in a Catholic high school or parish may call members of the community to gather and pray together. This service may also be used to precede an extended faculty meeting or day of in-service training. With modification in some of the choices, it might be used as an Advent or Lent gathering prayer to start the day for those members of the community—young people and adults—who wish to attend. Perhaps there may be a local or community circumstance that prompts a gathering in prayer. Whatever the reason, this service provides a format that is based on that of the traditional morning prayer of the Church. It begins with an introductory verse that is followed by a hymn. Psalm 63 is an appropriate morning psalm. After the psalm and psalm prayer, there is a reading. Following the reading is the gospel canticle, the Canticle of Zechariah, which expresses praise for our redemption. Intercessions, the Lord's Prayer, and a dismissal conclude the service. Depending on the participants and the experiences of the community, some direction and explanation might be needed, especially in regard to the format. The psalm and canticle should always be sung. The opening hymn and reading can be changed to fit the appropriate liturgical season or circumstance (Advent, Lent, Christmas, etc.). If there are particular local needs, these are acknowledged in the intercessions. Additional psalms can also be included.

A communion rite has been included for those occasions when it is celebrated in particular communities. The outline followed here is from Sunday Celebration in the Absence of a Priest (June 2, 1989, National Conference of Catholic Bishops). Familiarize yourself with this document, other writings on the topic, and particularly local diocesan policy before distributing communion in the absence of a priest.

MINISTERS

Someone in the community familiar with the format of morning prayer should serve as presider. This person will give the introductions, lead the responses and prayers, and read the intercessions. An additional minister is needed as lector. If there is a desire to involve more participants, another person could be asked to lead the intercessions.

The beginning of the academic year is a good time to start looking at students whom you may want to train as lay leaders of prayer. Morning and evening prayers are a wonderful introduction.

If you have considered using liturgical movement, begin by working with someone who can move gracefully and prayerfully with an incense pot.

ENVIRONMENT

Depending on the time of the year, deference to the particular liturgical season is appropriate as to color used, as well as any additional enhancements. Candles should be lit and the Bible or Lectionary needs to be displayed.

It is time to work into a religious/youth ministry budget moneys for these services. A school or parish community may have a worthy cross and paschal candle, but what about a finely made incense pot (perhaps a project for the art department), stands of different levels for items to be placed on (a good project for the shop department), or colored fabrics for draping (from the home economics department)? Also think about asking the parent community for help in these things; the projects might become intergenerational work.

MUSIC

There are simple music suggestions here. Think about your needs and feel free to change music selections, except for Psalm 63 and the Canticle of Zachary (these are prescribed for morning prayer). Many times, morning prayer and the communion rite can be sung a cappella. This could also be a time to introduce new cantors into their ministry.

LITURGY CHECKLIST

❑ Lectionary or Bible, marked and in place
❑ Worship aids
❑ Candles, in place and lit
❑ Incense pot, incense resins (in incense boat?), charcoal (lit)

ORDER OF WORSHIP

INTRODUCTORY RITES

GREETING *Each person makes the sign of the cross on the mouth as the presider begins:*

Presider: **Lord, open my lips.**

All: **And my mouth will proclaim your praise.**

HYMN "Come, All You People," basics CD/CS2-#1, music book #26.
or: "The Summons," basics CD/CS2-#14, music book #39.

PSALMODY

Please be seated.

PSALM "Psalm 63: As Morning Breaks," basics CD/CS1-#6, music book #19.

PSALM PRAYER *All stand.*

**God,
you created the sun to bring light to our days.
We invite you to be with us
as we begin this new day and celebrate its possibilities.
Strengthen the work of our hands
so that all we do is done in your name. R/.**

If a communion rite is to be included with morning prayer, continue on page 21 with the Liturgy of the Word; if there is no communion rite, continue immediately below:

LITURGY OF THE WORD

READING James 2:14–17, *Lectionary* #740, 12; or as appointed for the day.

REFLECTIONS *Although it is normal for a period of silence to be observed, you may want to provide a short homily based on your reflection on these questions:*

Who has shown you faith?
How do you describe your faith today.
What obstacles are in your life that prevent you from serving the needs of others?

GOSPEL CANTICLE "Blessed Be the Lord," songs CD/CS-#4, music book #4.

All make the sign of the cross at the beginning of the canticle. The altar, then the presider and people, may be incensed.

INTERCESSIONS
Or: *Book of Blessings,*
p. 846–847

The sun brings light to our days
and the Son of God has given us the light of life
through his resurrection from the dead.
Let us pray as one family gathered in his name.

Jesus is the light of the world. That those who follow Jesus bring that light to the places that are in darkness, let us pray to the Lord: R/.

God has given us a new day. That we may use this day and all its possibilities to bring life and peace to those around us, let us pray to the Lord: R/.

The morning sun removes the darkness and fears of night. That we look to Jesus for hope in times of fear and discouragement, let us pray to the Lord: R/.

God's goodness blesses our days. That his presence strengthen all those who are in special need of his help today, let us pray to the Lord: R/.

Each day is an opportunity to begin anew. That the work we do today honors God's name, let us pray to the Lord: R/.

And for what else do we pray this day?
Add your own intentions. . . .

Gathering our prayers and praises into one,
we pray as Jesus taught us:

All: Our Father . . .

CONCLUDING RITE

DISMISSAL *If the presider is not ordained (crossing oneself):*
May the Lord bless us,
protect us from all evil
and bring us to everlasting life. R/.

CLOSING SONG
(OPTIONAL)

"Yes, Lord," songs CD/CS-#1, music book #1.

Use the following rite if a communion rite is to be included with morning prayer.

LITURGY OF THE WORD

READING 1 — *As appointed for the day.*

RESPONSORIAL PSALM — *As appointed for the day.*

[READING 2] — *As appointed for the day.*

GOSPEL ACCLAMATION — "Word of Truth and Life," basics CD/CS2-#6, music book #31.
During Lent: "Open Our Ears," basics CD/CS2-#5, music book #30.

GOSPEL — *As appointed for the day.*

HOMILY REFLECTIONS — *You may want to provide a short homily based on your reflection on these questions:*

Who has shown you faith?
How do you describe your faith today.
What obstacles are in your life that prevent you from serving the needs
  of others?

GOSPEL CANTICLE — "Blessed Be the Lord," songs CD/CS-#4, music book #4.

INTERCESSIONS
Or: *Book of Blessings,*
p. 846–847

**The sun brings light to our days
and the Son of God has given us the light of life
through his resurrection from the dead.
Let us pray as one family gathered in his name.**

Jesus is the light of the world. That those who follow Jesus bring that light to the places that are in darkness, let us pray to the Lord: R/.

God has given us a new day. That we may use this day and all its possibilities to bring life and peace to those around us, let us pray to the Lord: R/.

The morning sun removes the darkness and fears of night. That we look to Jesus for hope in times of fear and discouragement, let us pray to the Lord: R/.

God's goodness blesses our days. That his presence strengthen all those who are in special need of his help today, let us pray to the Lord: R/.

Each day is an opportunity to begin anew. That the work we do today honors God's name, let us pray to the Lord: R/.

And for what else do we pray this day?
Add your own intentions. . . .

[Father,
we ask you to hear our prayers this day
as we pray in Jesus' name. R/.]

COMMUNION RITE

LORD'S PRAYER

SIGN OF PEACE

INVITATION TO
COMMUNION

COMMUNION SONG
"Psalm 34: Taste and See," basics CD/CS1-#7, music book #20.
Always observe some silence after Communion.

CONCLUDING PRAYER
Or: *Book of Blessings,*
p. 849, F #2005;
or from *Holy Communion
Outside of Mass.*

God, creator of all good things,
inspire and direct the work that we do today.
Strengthen us
so that everything we do is done in your name
and in the name of Jesus, your Son,
whose victory over death brings light to our lives.

We ask this through Jesus Christ our Lord. R/.

CONCLUDING RITE

GREETING AND
BLESSING
If the presider is not ordained (crossing oneself):
May the Lord bless us,
protect us from all evil
and bring us to everlasting life.

DISMISSAL
Go in the peace of Christ. R/.

CLOSING SONG
(OPTIONAL)
"Yes, Lord," songs CD/CS-#1, music book #1.

PREPARATION FOR MORNING PRAYER

GIVE THE GIFT OF A NEW DAY

DATE: **TIME:**

LOCATION:

OVERALL THEME   Faith in action.

SCRIPTURE USED   *[Please fill in for your specific celebration.]*

SHORT REFLECTION   Morning prayer is a traditional prayer of the Church. Having woken from slumber, we praise God for a new day. We pray that any word we may speak will praise God. We sing Psalm 63 (As morning breaks we praise you). We listen to Scripture; we sing a canticle of praise; and then we pray for the needs of the world. What is wonderful about this prayer is that it is prayed by people throughout the world. It is at these times that we help young people realize that they are part of the universal Church.

QUESTIONS FOR STUDENTS TO PONDER
1. Who in this school (parish) community shows us faith and prayer?
2. What forms of prayer do you use?
3. Who in our community is in need of our prayer?
4. How do you see yourself in relation with the Church throughout the world?

CLOSING COMMENTS   The Eucharist (Mass) is not the only time we pray. May you be able to join with your peers to share God's word and praise God for the gift of a new day.

Any questions, please contact _____.

PRAYER SERVICE OF JUSTICE
FOR TEAMS AND ENSEMBLES
ANYTIME THROUGHOUT THE SCHOOL YEAR

PREPARATION

GETTING STARTED

Justice, in and around school and the parish, plays an important role in the lives of our young people. Team playing is a way to justice. Often our athletic teams are called to act with virtue. Athletics and other "team" activities (speech, debate, band, chorus) play an important role in high schools. Being part of a team for some young men and women is one of the more significant aspects of their high school experience. Because hours are spent together in practices, games, travel, and competitions, members of a team or ensemble become, in one sense, a family for their season. In the Catholic school or parish program, the role of prayer in regard to teamwork may often be relegated to a quick invocation before each event. This service may help coaches and directors bridge the gap that might exist between the various competitive events and the spiritual-liturgical life of the school or parish community. The focus of the service does not center on praying for victory; it celebrates the health and strength and skill and talents of the young men and women, and calls upon God to bless their efforts. Depending on where in the season this prayer service is used, it may also provide an opportunity to celebrate and acknowledge the importance of teamwork.

This service could be used at the beginning of the season, once the team or ensemble is chosen and before the first event takes place. It might also be appropriate before a major competition or at the end of the season. Since the focus of this service is on the coaches, directors, and team or ensemble members, whoever is leading the service may wish to personalize it to the group and the occasion.

Because the group may be small, perhaps invite support people, other staff members, and families. As much participation from the team or ensemble as possible is desirable. Instead of designating someone to speak after the gospel, the coach or director (or campus minister if the coach or director is not comfortable) could share some of his or her reflections relative to the situation. These might be in the form of goals set, worked for, or achieved. After a short reflection, the team members could be invited to participate in this shared "homily." Ideally, students will be willing to share their thoughts.

MINISTERS

Since the intended group for whom this service is written is likely to be small in number, all ministers should be chosen from this group. Ideally, the leader should be the leader of the group, but if he or she is not comfortable, the campus minister might assist—or depending on the particular group of participants, one of them might be willing and capable of serving as leader of prayer. Ask members of the team to serve as lector and intercessor. So that things flow smoothly, giving the students the readings and intercessions ahead of time to practice is necessary. In smaller groups it is important that everyone be invited to add his or her own intentions aloud during the prayers of the faithful.

ENVIRONMENT

The ideal location for this service would be a place of prayer: the school chapel or prayer room. If that is not possible or there is no such facility on campus, students can gather in an empty classroom. If gathering at a large church, find a space that is small enough so all may be heard. The use of candles and the Bible would be most appropriate. The participants themselves could be asked to bring the candles to help personalize the service for them. Having the group sit in a circle would further enhance the team concept.

MUSIC

Music should be simple; so often when young people gather in a small group they are inhibited. Some of the songs would work well unaccompanied or perhaps with just a percussion background.

LITURGY CHECKLIST

☐ Copies of readings and intercessions
☐ Copies of the service for the participants
☐ Candles
☐ Bible or Lectionary

ORDER OF WORSHIP

INTRODUCTORY RITES

GATHERING SONG   "Come and Fill Our Hearts," basics CD/CS2-#9, music book #34.

GREETING

Presider: In the name of the Father, the Son, and Holy Spirit. R/.

God our creator, you are the source of all life and goodness.
Blessed be God forever.

All: Blessed be God forever.

Jesus, we look to you for hope in difficult times.
Blessed be God forever.

All: Blessed be God forever.

Holy Spirit, your presence gave the disciples courage.
Blessed be God forever.

All: Blessed be God forever.

OPENING PRAYER   Loving and faithful God,
we praise and thank you
for the ability to enjoy life and each other.
We call upon you to be with us
as we gather together (to begin this season).
We know that each of us as individuals
must be dedicated and work hard.
We also know how important it is
to respect and appreciate each other's gifts
as members of this team (ensemble).
Help us achieve the goals we have set
and support our efforts with your loving presence.

We ask all of these things in the name of Jesus, your Son,
who lives and reigns with you and the Holy Spirit,
one God, for ever and ever. R/.

LITURGY OF THE WORD

READING 1   1 Corinthians 9:16–19; 22–27, *Lectionary #441*
Always observe some silence after the reading.

PSALM "Psalm 103: Deep Down in My Soul, basics CD/CS1-#5, music book #18. *Observe some silence after the psalm.*

GOSPEL ACCLAMATION "Word of Truth and Life," basics CD/CS2-#6, music book #31.
During Lent: "Open Our Ears," basics CD/CS2-#5, music book #30.

GOSPEL Luke 8:16–18, *Lectionary #449*

HOMILY/ REFLECTION NOTES: *The person preparing the reflection might want to consider the following questions:*

What does "run so as to win" mean to you?
What kinds of things do people in competitions deny themselves?
Why is it important to set goals?
What do you hear in the passages from Scripture? (Allow others to share their experiences.)

RITUAL *Instrumentalists may play* "Come and Fill Our Hearts," *basics CD/CS2-#9, music book #34 during the ritual.*

I invite each member to come forward and have his or her palms signed.

The presider makes the sign of the cross in the open palms of each member, saying each time:

**May your hands be hands of justice,
may your work be filled with virtue,
and may your lives be formed by your goodness and kindness.**

GENERAL INTERCESSIONS Or: "Prayer of the Faithful," basics CD/CS2-#10, music book #10. *Be sure to add any intentions that are pertinent to your community.*

Presider: **God, guide for each of us here,
we ask you to listen to our needs
and answer our prayers for ourselves and those we love.**

Intercessor: **That the members of the team (ensemble) be blessed with good health and safety throughout the season, let us pray to the Lord: R/.**

For the coaches (director) and all the adults that assist with the program, let us pray to the Lord: R/.

For the parents who give up time and energy to support their sons and daughters: that they may be blessed with peaceful hearts, let us pray to the Lord: R/.

That the efforts of this team (ensemble) be blessed with success and good relationships, let us pray to the Lord: R/.

Please add your own intentions out loud.

Presider: **Almighty God,**
we ask your continued blessings and help.
Hear our prayers
and be with us now and all the days of our lives.
We ask this in the name of Jesus. R/.

LORD'S PRAYER *Join hands and pray together.*

SIGN OF PEACE **Let us offer each other a sign of peace and support.**

CONCLUDING PRAYER **Gentle God,**
Or: *Book of Blessings,* **we ask you to bless these young people with good health in**
p. 438, #1029 **their activities.**
Reward their efforts with success,
knowing that they have done their best.
Help them to support each other
both as friends and teammates.
Bless all of those involved in our programs,
including our families and friends.

We ask this through Christ our Lord. R/.

DISMISSAL **May the Lord bless us,**
protect us from all evil,
and bring us to everlasting life. R/.

CONCLUDING SONG "We Are Called," songs CD/CS #6, music book #6.
Or: "Blessed Be the Lord," songs CD/CS #4, music book #4.

PREPARATION FOR PRAYER SERVICE OF JUSTICE

GIVE THE GIFTS OF JUSTICE AND VIRTUE

DATE: **TIME:**

LOCATION:

OVERALL THEME   A celebration of talent and teamwork.

SCRIPTURE USED   1 Corinthians 9:16–19; 22–27 / Luke 8:16–18

SHORT REFLECTION   In many schools, extracurricular activities are an integral part of school (parish) life. They have a somewhat different focus because not only are they beyond the scope of the curriculum but the members of the team function as representatives of the school (parish) as they go from event to event. In some areas, extracurricular activities may even seem to take on a life of their own. By including more formal prayer into the rhythm of a competition season, this piece of school (parish) life becomes more intimately connected to the school (parish) mission and its spiritual life. Although this service may be held within a small group specific to a discipline, it is still important for the school (parish) community to know that these services are being held.

Though there may be hastily mumbled prayers before the competition begins, this service enhances the prayer life of the team or ensemble. In the context of a prayer service, the students have a chance to express gratitude for their strength, abilities, and talents. It also reminds them to work to the best of their ability so the whole group can shine. Praying together can help them refocus their attention and energies from themselves onto the group.

QUESTIONS FOR STUDENTS TO PONDER: Consider the line from the first reading: what does it mean to "run as to win"? Why is it important for individuals and teams (ensembles) to have goals? What kinds of things get in the way of true teamwork? What does a team (ensemble) really working together "look" like? What kinds of actions increase teamwork?

CLOSING COMMENTS   By connecting extracurricular activities to the prayer life of the community, the competitions of the students are enhanced and seen as an extension of justice and virtue. Without minimizing the importance of success, we celebrate teamwork and praise God for the talents and abilities of the individuals.

Any questions, please contact _____.

EUCHARISTIC CELEBRATION OF CLASS UNITY

ANYTIME IN THE SCHOOL YEAR

PREPARATION

GETTING STARTED

The four years of high school are often marked by milestone events that are typical to all high school students—driver's license, first job, first formal dance, turning sixteen, taking the ACT; however, each school has its own events that become part of the tradition and culture. For many Catholic schools, one of these is the ring ceremony or liturgy that surrounds the reception and blessing of the school rings. Depending on the size of the school, rings may actually be received at the liturgy; this ritual could also take place at a parish youth liturgy. Another special milestone that students often refer to as their most meaningful high-school experience is the class or youth ministry retreat. Both of these events, especially the ring ceremony, provide opportunities to bring in the faith dimension—celebrating unity and oneness in and through the person of Jesus. The elements of this service are intended to center on that unity and togetherness. Within this liturgy, friendship is celebrated as well. For the entrance procession, in addition to the processional cross, class officers or peer ministers should each carry a candle.

For further background for blessing of articles, see "Order for a Blessing to Be Used in Various Circumstances" found in *Book of Blessings*, p. 841–851, #1984–2011, and "Order for the Blessing of Religious Articles," p. 617–624.

MINISTERS

Since the liturgy focuses on the members of the class in a special way, as much as possible, those who have a visible role in the service should have been participants in the retreat or members of the class. The class officers or peer ministers will carry the candles. If there are no members of the group who are eucharistic ministers, those who are in some way involved with this group should perform this ministry (adults or other students). You may also want to ask peer ministers of the parish to take roles.

ENVIRONMENT

It is important to include any symbols or banners that are important to this group or their experiences together. Depending on the size of the group, the liturgy may be held in a smaller space or one not usually used for Mass. Involve the members of the class or group in enhancing the space.

MUSIC

This should be a liturgy of great joy. The gathering song and penitential rite are connected. Consider a procession to the place for liturgy. If this is a retreat liturgy, it would be wonderful to have the retreatants join an assembly already singing.

The closing song, "Canticle of the Turning," moves quickly. Keep it going that way. You may want to use dancers to lead a procession to another space where a special celebration (a meal?) would be shared.

LITURGY CHECKLIST

- ❏ Copies of readings, given to readers in advance
- ❏ Copy of intercessions, given to intercessor in advance
- ❏ Vestments for presider
- ❏ Lectionary, marked and in place
- ❏ Sacramentary and Book of Blessings, marked and in place
- ❏ Processional cross in place
- ❏ Candles, in place and lit
- ❏ Class representative or peer ministry candles, in place and lit
- ❏ Banners and banner stands (or other class symbols) in place
- ❏ Bread, wine, water, ciboria and communion cups, corporal, purificator(s), finger bowl, finger towel
- ❏ Incense pot, incense resins (in incense boat?), charcoal (lit)
- ❏ Worship aids distributed
- ❏ All involved in the procession are in place—lector, intercessor, banner carriers, class representatives, any assistants, presider

Other:

ORDER OF WORSHIP

INTRODUCTORY RITES

GATHERING SONG

"Send Down the Fire," basics CD/CS2-#2, music book #27.
Instrumentalists continue song throughout greeting and into penitential version.

GREETING

PENITENTIAL RITE
Or: *Sacramentary*, p. 360
(406), invitation B,
C-iv (c-4)

The early followers of Jesus gave us the example of what it meant
    to live together in unity.
Christians are called to love one another,
which is how people recognized who they were.
Jesus reached out in compassion to others
and expected his friends to do the same.
For all the times that we as a class
have let down each other as members of this community
    and as friends,
let us ask forgiveness.

"Send Down the Fire (Penitential rite)," basics CD/CS2-#3, music book #28.
Or: "I confess to almighty God…"

May almighty God have mercy on us,
forgive us our sins,
and bring us to everlasting life. R/.

OPENING PRAYER
Or: *Sacramentary*,
p. 889 (806), #13-A,
For Unity of Christians

Let us pray.

God, eternal friend and guide,
we know how important it is
to surround ourselves with good friends
who will support us in the ways that matter.
Be with us in this special time of our lives
as we celebrate the gifts that each person brings.
Bless our friends
and keep them safe on their journey.

We ask this through our Lord Jesus Christ, your Son,
who lives and reigns with you and the Holy Spirit,
one God, for ever an ever. R/.

LITURGY OF THE WORD

READING 1 Colossians 3:9–17, *Lectionary #812-6*
Always observe some silence after the reading.

PSALM "Psalm 104: Lord, Send Out Your Spirit," basics CD/CS1-#11, music book #24.
Observe some silence after the psalm.

GOSPEL ACCLAMATION "Word of Truth and Life," basics CD/CS2-#6, music book #31.
You may wish to incense the gospel. See the appendix for suggestions.

GOSPEL John 17:20–26, *Lectionary #815-8*

HOMILY/ REFLECTION NOTES *If the presider is not a member of the community, it might be more appropriate to have one of the members of the class or someone more closely affiliated with the group speak. Some questions to consider:*

What have been some of the milestones, transforming experiences,
    in your own life?
What are the situations in your life in which you have experienced unity
    and togetherness with a group?
How do these experiences strengthen faith?
How do the words of the Gospel about being one in God the Father and
    Jesus relate to your experiences?

RITUAL *After the homily, especially if this liturgy marks the reception of the class rings, it would be appropriate for the presider to bless the rings as adapted from the Book of Blessings (see Getting Started notes).*

**Blessed be your name, O Lord,
you are the fount and source of every blessing,
and you look with delight
upon the devout practices of the faithful.
Draw near, we pray, to these your servants
and, as they use this symbol of their faith and devotion,
grant that they may also strive to be transformed
into the likeness of Christ, your Son,
who lives and reigns with you for ever and ever. R/.**

GENERAL INTERCESSIONS Or: "Prayer of the Faithful," basics CD/CS2-#10, music book #35.
Be sure to add any intentions that are pertinent to your community. The intercessor should be in place before the presider gives the invitation to pray. These prayers may be led from the ambo.

Presider: **Loving God,
we now extend our prayers beyond our class community
    to those in need**

and to all those we love.

Intercessor: For our church and all who share faith, let us prayer to the Lord: R/.

For those who lead us in ways of unity, let us pray to the Lord: R/.

For all young people who struggle to find their way: that they find someone to assist and support them in their search, let us pray to the Lord: R/.

For the families of the members of this class: that they are able to share in the joy and faith at this special time, let us pray to the Lord: R/.

For our friends of yesterday, today, and tomorrow, who bring us love and laughter, let us pray to the Lord: R/.

For the members of the Class of ____, who share this special time: that faith in God continue to unite them, let us pray to the Lord: R/.

Other intentions may be added here.

For the people we love who have died: that one day we meet again in God's presence, let us pray to the Lord: R/.

The intercessor should face the presider and not leave until the prayer is finished.

Presider: **Loving God,**
we count on you to hear us
and answer our prayers through Jesus,
who lives for ever and ever. R/.

LITURGY OF THE EUCHARIST

PREPARATION OF THE ALTAR AND THE GIFTS   "I Say Yes, My Lord," songs CD/CS-#10, music book #10.
Class representatives present the gifts of bread and wine.

PRAYER OVER THE GIFTS
Or: *Sacramentary*, p. 889
(806), #13-A,
For Unity of Christians   **Faithful God,**
take these gifts we offer
as a sign of the unity we celebrate.
Keep us together in the love and faith we share.
We ask this through Christ our Lord. R/.

EUCHARISTIC PRAYER   *Sacramentary*, p. 556 (517), Eucharistic Prayer IV
"Eucharistic Acclamations," basics CD/CS2-#11, music book #36.

COMMUNION RITE

LORD'S PRAYER

SIGN OF PEACE

BREAKING OF THE BREAD
"Lamb of God," basics CD/CS2-#12, music book #37.
Ask the other ministers to help break bread and pour wine so this rite will not be extended.

COMMUNION SONG
"For Living, for Dying," songs CD/CS-#5, music book #5.
Always observe some silence after Communion.

PRAYER AFTER COMMUNION
Or: *Sacramentary,* p. 889 (806), #13-A, For Unity of Christians

Let us pray.

Almighty God,
we celebrate our unity in faith
by receiving your Son in Communion.
Let this holy communion
keep us together in faith and friendship.

We ask this through Christ our Lord. R/.

CONCLUDING RITE

GREETING AND BLESSING
Or: *Book of Blessings,* p. 849, #2004

The presider invites the class members forward and prays over them.

Holy God, who has gathered us,
we call upon you to bless these young men and women on this special day.
They come holding dreams of their futures in their hands and hearts.
Bless them with joyful and loving hearts.
Lift them up when they are discouraged.
Inspire them when they become overwhelmed with the stress of high school.
Above all,
may they know that they are never alone;
that you are with them always. R/.

The presider then blesses the assembly.
Or: *Book of Blessings,* p. 851, #2009
Or: "Blessing," basics CD/CS2-#16, music book #41.

May the God of laughter bring joy to your days. R/.
May Jesus our friend support you in your difficult times. R/.

May the Spirit of hope challenge you to continue to reach for your dreams. R/.

May the almighty God bless you, the Father, and the Son, ✠ and the Holy Spirit. R/.

DISMISSAL

RECESSIONAL SONG   "He Came Down / We Are Marching (Siyahumba)," basics CD/CS1-#2, music book #15.
Process to post-Liturgy celebration.

PREPARATION FOR EUCHARISTIC CELEBRATION OF CLASS UNITY

GIVE THE GIFT OF CLASS UNITY

DATE: **TIME:**

LOCATION:

OVERALL THEME   Celebrating our friendship and unity in the Lord.

SCRIPTURE USED   Colossians 3:9–17 / John 17:20–26

SHORT REFLECTION: The time of closing a retreat or marking the reception of class rings presents an opportunity to focus on how our faith brings us together. Friendships are integral to the high school experience; this liturgy extends that togetherness to all members of a particular class or to those who have shared a retreat together. The most important high school memories are those that bring groups together in significant ways. Here is the chance to bring our shared beliefs into that equation. This is a milestone that focuses on a shared experience whose power can go a long way to generating positive feelings and attitudes within the group.

QUESTIONS FOR STUDENTS TO PONDER
1. What kinds of events have brought this class together?
2. What does the class ring (retreat, etc.) mean to you as a member of this class? This school?
3. What are the most special moments you have shared with friends?
4. What made those times so significant?
5. What can we do to extend the sense of oneness beyond this day or this time?

CLOSING COMMENTS   It is easy to find the unity in a retreat or ring ceremony. Some guidance and assistance will be needed to help teens focus on the role of faith and the unity they share in the presence of God.

Any questions, please contact _____.

EUCHARISTIC COMMISSIONING SERVICE OF SCHOOL/GROUP LEADERSHIP

ANYTIME IN THE SCHOOL YEAR

PREPARATION

GETTING STARTED

It would be the unusual school that did not have some form of student government in place—student council, class council, class officers. Many parishes may have youth groups with elected leaders. The election of these young people to their respective positions is an essential part of high school life. Depending on the size of the school and local traditions, this may be surrounded by a good deal of fanfare with an induction and local publicity, or nothing at all. This part of life in a high school provides yet another opportunity to see what is viewed as a nonreligious event in the context of faith. Instead of viewing elections as a popularity contest, elected students can see them as a mandate from their peers and as a call to serve their constituency in some leadership capacity for the school year. Through the use of a prayer service to surround the election and induction, the entire school community can be gathered to celebrate the commissioning of these young people, who were called forth from the student body. The readings selected focus on the aspect of call. We hear Jeremiah's protest of not being entirely qualified—students may be able to identify with this feeling of unreadiness. In the gospel, we hear the familiar call of Matthew to follow Jesus. This may seem like a stretch to connect student elections with the call of the prophets and apostles, but not if we remind them that inherent in leadership is the call to serve. It is helpful for adolescents to see these positions of leadership in the school community as an extension of their baptismal call. This service should include the distribution of any symbols of leadership—certificates or pins or whatever else is part of the culture. Included also is a prayer of commissioning with parts for those being commissioned and for the response of the community.

When adapting the service for a parish setting, you may want to celebrate a liturgy during which the community recognizes the leaders of all student organizations—everything from cheerleaders, to band officers, to leaders of drama troupes. Let them realize they are to serve not only their peers but the community as well with justice and dignity.

MINISTERS

The presider for this prayer service should ideally be someone who knows and is known to the student body so that he or she is familiar with the culture of the community. If this is not possible, at least the person who offers the reflection should be part of the community—the principal, the moderator of the student government organization, the campus minister, or the parish youth minister. Since new officers or student representatives are being commissioned, it might be appropriate for those who held these offices in the previous year to take on the roles of readers and participants in the entrance procession; the new officers might serve to bring up gifts and/or prepare the altar at the preparation of the gifts. It provides both groups with visibility and acknowledges the service of the previous leaders. The adult leadership of the school should also have part in the service in some way.

ENVIRONMENT

The use of school or parish colors and banners is important in this service. If the student government or youth ministry has its own symbols, these should be part of the environment as well. Enough chairs should be set up in the area of focus so that all ministers in the service can be seated.

MUSIC

This is a special time—the texts should speak of awe, wonder, and how the Holy spirit interacts with the youth in roles of leadership. The music needs to be festive. The gathering song and the Gloria suggested here are based on the same melody. During Communion use a psalm that may not need a worship aid for participation, but which can be sung with a "spirit" of a soulful journey. The dismissal song is one of a great yes. Listen to the recording for ideas of how to "let loose." It is a 16-year-old who sang those parts—and his first time in a recording studio. Let the students have a personal experience with the music!

LITURGY CHECKLIST

- ❑ Copies of readings, given to readers in advance
- ❑ Copy of intercessions, given to intercessor in advance
- ❑ Vestments for presider
- ❑ Lectionary, marked and in place
- ❑ Sacramentary, marked and in place
- ❑ Processional cross in place
- ❑ Candles, in place and lit
- ❑ Banners and banner stands in place
- ❑ Bread, wine, water, ciboria and communion cups, corporal, purificator(s), finger bowl, finger towel
- ❑ Symbols of leadership to be presented, in place
- ❑ Worship aids distributed
- ❑ All involved in the procession are in place—lector, intercessor, banner carriers, those to be commissioned, administration representatives (if any), presider

Other:

ORDER OF WORSHIP

INTRODUCTORY RITES

GATHERING SONG

"He Came Down / We Are Marching (Siyahumba)," basics CD/CS1-#2, music book #15.
The song may need to be shortened for the processional in some settings. The instrumentalists should continue through to the Gloria.

GREETING

We assemble as a community of faith
to recognize the call to leadership
being accepted by these young men and women.
In our prayers today,
we remember all those who have served this community.
Let us pray that God be with them
and all of us
as we continue to live out the call
to be followers of Jesus.

PENITENTIAL RITE
Or: *Sacramentary*, p. 360
(406), invitation B,
C-iv (c-4)

It is not always easy to live up to
what others expect of us
or we expect of ourselves.

Jesus, you taught us the meaning of service when you washed the feet
of your friends:
Lord, have mercy. R/.

Jesus, you never turned down a request for help or healing:
Christ, have mercy. R/.

Jesus, you accepted all people and challenged them to be their
best selves.
Lord, have mercy. R/.

May almighty God have mercy on us,
forgive us our sins,
and bring us to everlasting life. R/.

GLORIA

"Glory to God," basics CD/CS1-#3, music book #16.

OPENING PRAYER
Or: *Sacramentary*, p. 898
(812), #16, For Pastoral or
Spiritual Meetings,
alternative opening prayer

Let us pray.

Almighty God,
you gave us your Son, Jesus,
to show us what it meant to serve others.
He washed the feet of his friends
and never turned down anyone in need.
We ask you to help us,
and especially those who will be commissioned today,
to be people who take our call to serve seriously.

We ask all of this through our Lord Jesus Christ, your Son,
who lives and reigns with you and the Holy Spirit,
one God, for ever and ever. R/.

LITURGY OF THE WORD

READING 1

Jeremiah 1:4–9, *Lectionary #719-7*
Always observe some silence after the reading.

PSALM

"Psalm 118: This Is the Day," basics CD/CS1-#9, music book #22.
Observe some silence after the psalm.

GOSPEL ACCLAMATION

"Word of Truth and Life," basics CD/CS2-#6, music book #31.

GOSPEL

Matthew 9:9–13, *Lectionary #643*

HOMILY/ REFLECTION NOTES

As you prepare your reflection, you may want to consider the following questions:
When have you felt inadequate or incapable of carrying out a task
  or responsibility?
What do you do when you feel that you are just not up to the job?
What situations make it hard to just "pick up and follow"?
How do you understand the idea of servant-leader?

RITUAL

The presider or school principal leads this part of the service and begins by addressing
those to be commissioned by asking them to stand.

Presider:

Each one of you has been called forth by this community
to serve as leaders to your peers for this school year.
This involves acting as their representative and voice.
As leaders, you are also challenged to respond
    to the call to be of service.
Do you accept this challenge?

Student Leaders:

We do.

Presider: This call to be leaders asks you to be sensitive to the needs of
your peers
and at the same time to uphold the mission of the school (parish) in
the decisions you make.
Are you willing to do this?

Students Leaders: We are.

Accept these symbols of leadership
as you begin your year of service.

Distribute pins or certificates or Scriptures.

I invite the assembly to stand
and extend their hands in blessing over our new officers (leaders).

Or: "Blessing," basics CD/CS2-#16, music book #41.

Let us raise our hands in a gesture of blessing over the newly
commissioned leaders.

God,
we call upon you to bless the work of our hands.
Bless in a special way
those who have been called to serve as leaders of our school (parish).
Give them courage to act with justice
and make decisions for the good of all the members of this
community.
Bless each one of us with your love and presence.

We ask this through Christ our Lord. R/.

Let us welcome our new leaders.
Applause of affirmation.

GENERAL
INTERCESSIONS
Presider:

Or: "Prayer of the Faithful," basics CD/CS2-#10, music book #35.

God our creator,
we look to you to help us be
the persons you want and need us to be.
Hear our prayers for all those in need.

Intercessor: For the leaders of the world, our nation, our city and our Church:
that they may see their call to lead as one of serving the needs of all,
let us pray to the Lord: R/.

For the leaders this school community: that the Spirit of wisdom and
courage guide their actions and decisions, let us pray to the Lord: R/.

For those who led our student government last year, let us pray to the
Lord: R/.

For those newly commissioned to school leadership: that God bless their efforts this year, let us pray to the Lord: R/.

For all those who have died: that their example in this life lead us one day to follow them into God's presence, let us pray to the Lord: R/.

Presider: Loving God,
hear the prayers of those who call upon you
in Jesus' name. R/.

LITURGY OF THE EUCHARIST

PREPARATION OF THE ALTAR AND THE GIFTS

"The Summons," basics CD/CS2-#14, music book #39.
Students who are assigned bring forward the gifts of bread, water, and wine.

PRAYER OVER THE GIFTS
Or: *Sacramentary*, p. 898 (812), #16, For Pastoral and Spiritual Meetings

God of all living things,
may these gifts be a humble offering to you
as we offer ourselves in leadership.
May these gifts and our lives be blessed for ever.

We ask this through Christ our Lord. R/.

EUCHARISTIC PRAYER

Sacramentary, p. 548 (504), Eucharistic Prayer II
"Eucharistic Acclamations," basics CD/CS2-#11, music book #36.

COMMUNION RITE

LORD'S PRAYER

SIGN OF PEACE

BREAKING OF THE BREAD

"Lamb of God," basics CD/CS2-#12, music book #37.
Ask the other ministers to help break bread and pour wine so this rite will not be extended.

COMMUNION SONG

"Psalm 34: Taste and See," basics CD/CS1-#7, music book #20.
Always observe some silence after Communion.

PRAYER AFTER COMMUNION
Or: *Sacramentary*, p. 898 (812), #16, For Pastoral and Spiritual Meetings

Let us pray.

Good and gracious God,
may the food we have shared
fill our lives and open our hearts
to your call for leadership.

We ask this through Jesus, your Son. R/.

CONCLUDING RITE

GREETING AND BLESSING Or: "Blessing," basics CD/CS2-#16, music book #41.
Or: *Sacramentary*, p.570 (529), #3, Beginning of the New Year

DISMISSAL

RECESSIONAL SONG "Yes, Lord," songs CD/CS-#1, music book #1.

PREPARATION FOR EUCHARISTIC COMMISSIONING SERVICE OF SCHOOL/GROUP LEADERSHIP

GIVE THE GIFT OF LEADERSHIP

DATE: **TIME:**

LOCATION:

OVERALL THEME   Acknowledging our call to serve.

SCRIPTURE USED   Jeremiah 1:4–9 / Matthew 9:9–13

SHORT REFLECTION   The commissioning of school or youth ministy leaders invites the entire community to gather and celebrate the gifts of those elected. It also provides an opportunity to recognize this leadership in the context of the call to be of service to others. As baptized Christians, we all realize that call, but this time in a teen's life invites us to focus on the service role that student leaders are asked to assume within the community. Certainly, not everyone makes themselves available to run for office, but those that do are already putting themselves on the line in front of their peers. By reflecting on the call of Jeremiah and Matthew in the readings for this service, the school is asked to look at these leadership positions from another perspective. Though these positions bring with them some prestige, emphasizing call and service weaves into the induction, or commissioning, what is at the heart of the Christian message. This might also provide an opportunity to look at the school's mission and the responsibility of school leaders to support it.

QUESTIONS FOR STUDENTS TO PONDER
1. What are the ways in which leadership and service go together?
2. Why is it sometimes hard to accept a mandate or call from peers for you to lead or stand apart from the group? (Jeremiah reading)
3. In what ways are you able to demonstrate support for the student leaders?
4. What aspects of the school mission do you think are in need of support by our newly elected student leaders?

CLOSING COMMENTS   Each one of us by the virtue of our baptism is called to serve. Some among us are called to do it in a more visible way. This does not imply that those who are called forth from the community are any better or worse than the rest. They accept the call to serve, realize the responsibility it involves, and depend on the support of the group to fulfill their leadership position.

Any questions, please contact _____.

COMMISSIONING SERVICE FOR COMMUNITY SERVICE

ANYTIME IN THE SCHOOL YEAR

PREPARATION

GETTING STARTED

High school life is bound to include a certain number of service clubs, organizations, or community service opportunities. Many schools—public and private—and parish religious education programs have even mandated service hours or programs as a graduation requirement. This service may or may not be done within the school itself and may involve a good deal of outreach into the surrounding community. Other forms of service include participating in a liturgical choir or instrumental ensemble; still another might extend to those who take a more active role in school liturgies and prayer services as lectors, eucharistic ministers, ushers, or preparation assistants. Depending on the structure of the school, these groups might be formal or informal in nature. Whatever approach an individual school (or parish) takes to incorporate these many forms of service into its communal life, by having a formal commissioning or recognition the community says that the service performed by these groups is important and worthy of acknowledgment in a public manner. We do this in a prayer service that both celebrates the service and commissions those who serve. In order to make this prayer experience applicable to a number of situations, it remains general in nature. If your service specifically commissions liturgical ministries, reference the Book of Blessings (chapters 61, 62, 63) for prayers that are more specific to replace the ones suggested here.

The readings focus on the idea of service—the sending forth of the apostles and utilizing our gifts for the service of all. In general, it can be difficult to recruit or sell teens on the idea of free-will service at a time in their lives when tangible rewards gain in significance—good grades for hard work; money earned at a part-time job. Thus, a public celebration in the context of prayer may serve as reminder of the call we received at baptism to follow in the footsteps of Jesus as one who came to serve, not to be served.

MINISTERS

Most likely, those performing the ministries in this service are also those being celebrated and commissioned. A lector, a reader for the intercessions, those who will carry the cross and candles, and anyone being acknowledged at this service should be involved in the entrance procession. This is appropriate unless the group attending is very small or the number being commissioned is very large. Ideally, the presider is linked to the life of the community, particularly in the service arena, whether as campus minister, service coordinator, youth minister, or school administrator. If there is a priest on campus and he is the one who is involved with the students in this capacity, then he should preside. Since this liturgy acknowledges the students who provide the service, perhaps one of the juniors or seniors should offer a reflection on his or her experience as a response to the readings. It would also be fitting to have one of the youths speak about one of the services in which they are involved.

ENVIRONMENT

Create wordless banners with images of service needs. These can be hung around school or church during the year. The use of water to enhance the blessing requires a bowl of water and a suitable aspergill for sprinkling.

MUSIC

Service is the word for the day. The texts of the music should inspire us and move us toward service. Beginning with "Now" creates an urgency that we must help others, for we are all part of this world community. Continue with the penitential rite based on the same musical themes. Psalm 23 is appropriate for a responsorial psalm, since we are being asked to do more than just serve: we must also invite others to the table. "If" after the commissioning ceremony can be a powerful conclusion: it has been known to help open hardened hearts to the power of the freely given service of youth. Do not hesitate to conclude with "Holy Ground," even if the community is unaccustomed to singing Spanish; let them learn the few required responses in the song. The music unites us with those who may seem foreign to us—as acts of service also do!

LITURGY CHECKLIST

- ❑ Copies of readings, given to readers in advance
- ❑ Copy of intercessions, given to intercessor in advance
- ❑ Alb for leader
- ❑ Lectionary, marked and in place
- ❑ Sacramentary, marked and in place
- ❑ Book of Blessing, marked and in place
- ❑ Processional cross in place
- ❑ Banners and stands in place
- ❑ Bowl of water and aspergill in place
- ❑ Candles, in place and lit
- ❑ Worship aids distributed
- ❑ All involved in the procession are in place—lector, intercessor, banner bearers, those to be commissioned, any assistants, presider

Other:

ORDER OF WORSHIP

INTRODUCTORY RITES

GATHERING SONG

"Now," songs CD/CS-#13, music book #13.
Instrumentalists may continue playing into the penitential rite.

GREETING
Or: *Book of Blessings,*
pp. 842–843, #1989–1990

As the presider makes the sign of the cross:
We gather in the name of God our creator, who gave us life.
We come together in the name of Jesus, whose whole life was
an example of service.
We pray in the presence of the Holy Spirit, our strength and wisdom. R/.

In this celebration
we raise our hearts and voices in prayer to God:
Creator, Son, and Spirit.
We are confident that our God hears us
as together we pray in a special way
for those who serve our community.
With the help of the Holy Spirit
we know that we can be the hands of Jesus
that reach out to others in our world today.

PENITENTIAL RITE

"Now (Penitential rite)," basics CD/CS2-#4, music book #29.

OPENING PRAYER
Or: *Sacramentary,* p. 882
(801), #8, For Ministers
of the Church

If the presider is ordained:
[Let us pray.]

Almighty God,
your Son, Jesus, gave us the example
of what it means to serve
when he washed the feet of his disciple
and in so many other ways while he was on earth.
It is sometimes hard to balance
all the things we have to do in our lives
and make time for others.
So we ask you to bless those
who are generous with their time and talents.
Support them in the service they perform
and help us to do the same.

We ask this through our Lord Jesus Christ, your Son,
who lives and reigns with you and the Holy Spirit,
one God, for ever and ever. R/.

LITURGY OF THE WORD

READING 1

1 Peter 4:7–11, *Lectionary* #770-13

PSALM   "Psalm 23: Shepherd Me, O God," basics CD/CS1-#10, music book #23.
Observe some silence after the psalm.

GOSPEL ACCLAMATION   "Word of Truth and Life," basics CD/CS2-#6, music book #31.
During Lent: "Open Our Ears," basics CD/CS2-#5, music book #30.

GOSPEL   Matthew 20:25–28, *Lectionary #773-4*

HOMILY/
REFLECTION NOTES
As you prepare your reflection, you may want to consider these questions. Also consider inviting one those involved in one of the service projects to share his or her experience as a part of your homily/reflection.

What impelled you to become involved in service to others?
Where do you get support to continue to be of service in a formal way?
What kinds of service do you do?
How do you make time for being involved and helping others?
What are the rewards involved in giving service?
Where does the message of today's gospel reading about "serving the needs of all" fit into your understanding of service?

RITUAL
**My brothers and sisters,
we know how hard it is sometimes
to live up to the call we received at baptism
and strengthened at confirmation.
We all try to do the best we can
to follow Jesus in our words and actions.
Today, we celebrate and send forth young men and women among us
who have been generous with their time and the gifts God has
given them
by sharing these gifts with others.**

We ask them to stand as we pray for them.

The presider calls each one by name to the front. Once all have assembled, the minister prays the following prayer over them. (An ordained minister says the prayer with arms outstretched and may bless with water. A lay minister prays with hands joined.)

**Lord,
let the effect of your blessing
remain with your faithful people
to give them new life and strength of spirit,
so that the power of your love
will enable them to accomplish what is right and good.**

We ask this through Christ our Lord. R/.

GENERAL
INTERCESSIONS
Presider:
Or: *Book of Blessings,*p. 846–847, #1997

God loved us so much

that he gave us his Son.
Because we believe in God's love for us,
we know that he will hear and answer our prayers.

Intercessor: Jesus came to serve not to be served. For all those who serve us in civil and government positions: that they may serve with integrity, let us pray to the Lord: R/.

Jesus sent his disciples out to serve the needs of all. For those who serve the neediest among us—the sick, the homeless, the lonely, the elderly: that God bless their generosity, let us pray to the Lord: R/.

God's gifts to us should be used at the service of one another. For the students among us who serve our school community as _____, let us pray to the Lord: R/.

Each of us has been called to serve others. For all of us: that we might be more generous with the gifts God has given to us and share them with others, let us pray to the Lord: R/.

Jesus met the needs of the people by teaching them. For the teachers and administrators in this school community: that they be blessed for their loving service, let us pray to the Lord: R/.

LORD'S PRAYER Let us bring our prayers to God
by praying as Jesus taught us to pray: R/.

SIGN OF PEACE

CONCLUDING RITE

BLESSING
Or: "Blessing,"
basics CD/CS2-#16,
music book #41.
Or: *Book of Blessings,*
p. 851, #2009, 2010

If the presider is ordained:
[The Lord be with you. R/.

Bow your heads and pray for God's blessing.

May our Lord Jesus Christ himself and God our Father,
who has loved us and has given us everlasting encouragement
and good hope through his grace,
comfort your hearts and make them strong
for every good deed and word. R/.

May almighty God bless you,
the Father, and the Son, ✠ and the Holy Spirit. R/.]

If the presider is not ordained (crossing oneself):
May the Lord bless us,
protect us from all evil
and bring us to everlasting life. R/.

CLOSING SONG "Holy Ground," songs CD/CS-#2, music book #2.

PREPARATION FOR COMMISSIONING
FOR COMMUNITY SERVICE

GIVE THE GIFT OF SERVICE TO OTHERS

DATE: **TIME:**

LOCATION:

OVERALL THEME   Celebrating and commissioning those who serve.

SCRIPTURE USED   1 Peter 4:7–11 / Matthew 20:25–28

SHORT REFLECTION   Oftentimes in our society it seems as if it is only the athletes or the award-winning scholars who achieve name recognition and publicity; those who offer their gifts, talents, and time at the service of others in a number of ways within or outside of the school community do so without fanfare. This service celebrates, in the context of prayer, the contributions of those who have taken to heart the mandate of Jesus to serve others. These may be liturgical ministers, those who do community outreach, those who tutor, etc. We all are called by baptism to follow this mandate, but these particular individuals are generous with their time in a way in which not all of us are. Not everyone is content with the less tangible rewards that come from serving others. The Gospel reminds us that the last shall be first; if you want to be great, you need to serve; if you rank first you must serve the needs of all. This is not an easy message to internalize or live out, so we take the time to bless and pray for those who have made service a part of their lives and acknowledge the importance of their contributions to this faith community.

QUESTIONS FOR STUDENTS TO PONDER
1. What talents and gifts do you have that can be used in the service of others?
2. What obstacles do you face as you consider offering service?
3. What about Jesus' message of service in the Gospel appeals to you the most?
4. What are some of the rewards that come from being of service to others?
5. How can you be supportive of those who do give special service to this community?

CLOSING COMMENTS   Not everyone has the same gifts; not all of us can be star athletes or come in at the top of our class in academics. But each one of us has unique gifts and talents from God. It is part of our call as baptized Christians that we share what we have with others and thus continue to build the community of faith.

Any questions, please contact _____.

EVENING PRAYER FOR EVENING MEETING
ANYTIME THROUGHOUT THE SCHOOL YEAR

PREPARATION

GETTING STARTED

Parents are an integral part of the Catholic high school community and ministry. Admittedly, their involvement is different from that of parents at the elementary school level, since it may be limited to parent-teacher conferences or include some volunteering. Assuming that schools and parishes do have some type of parent organization, and it does meet from time to time, it is appropriate to extend the school's prayer life to include them. A parents meeting, an open board meeting, a teen council meeting are all opportunities to begin with prayer. The service that follows is a celebration of evening prayer (vespers), which is part of the Church's long-standing tradition to mark the different hours, or parts, of the day with an official prayer. This can be used to begin any evening meeting. It includes prayer, psalms, a reading from Scripture, and intercessions. The psalms and canticle should be sung. Some introduction about the nature of evening prayer might be appropriate, depending on the group that is gathered. A comment referencing the above information might be all that is needed.

This prayer would also be very appropriate for gatherings of young people in the evening. Think about always beginning your gatherings with this traditional prayer of the Church. It has its own rhythm and can be adapted to many situations. The reproducible preparation page has been included for such occasions.

MINISTERS

There are few roles if this is a small gathering. Someone is needed to lead evening prayer, another to serve as assistant, and a third person to proclaim the reading. If incense is being used, the assistant can incense the ambo (or whatever lectern is bearing the Lectionary or Bible) and the congregation during the praying of Psalm 141. If the group is larger, an entrance procession with someone to carry the cross, candles, lectionary, and incense pot would invite more roles in the service. In addition, someone could be asked to lead the intercessions. If the community has student leaders of prayer, consider having them serve as the ministers of this service.

ENVIRONMENT

The worship space, large or small, could be enhanced by the use of candles and green plants. Again, much would depend on the size of the group and the location of the meeting. It would be appropriate for each member of the assembly to have a taper. Low lighting and use of incense can enhance the prayer experience by involving more of the senses. A large cross or sizable icon may serve as a focal point.

MUSIC

Traditional evening prayer music would be appropriate. The selections suggested here are simple and repetitive. Consider using a student cantor with simple accompaniment, perhaps a keyboard or guitar. During Advent, it would be appropriate to use "Come, O Come, Emmanuel / O Antiphons," basics CD/CS1-#1, music book #14, during the gathering and the procession of light. Since this prayer is traditionally sung, try to have the presider sing the blessing found on the recording and have the assembly repeat it.

LITURGY CHECKLIST

- ❑ Lectionary or Bible
- ❑ Book of Blessings
- ❑ Copies of the readings, intercession
- ❑ Paschal candle
- ❑ Incense pot, incense resins (in incense boat?), charcoal (lit) (if used)
- ❑ Tapers for all participants (if used)
- ❑ Copies of the service for everyone
- ❑ Processional cross and candles (if needed)

Other:

ORDER OF WORSHIP

INTRODUCTORY RITES

GREETING   We gather to give thanks to God for the day that is ending.
We look back on actions taken and words spoken
and lift them to God as we pray together.

Light and peace in Jesus Christ our Lord.

All: Thanks be to God.

OPENING HYMN   "The Summons," basics CD/CS2-#14, music book #39.
The light is passed from the paschal candle to the tapers during the opening song.

LITURGY OF THE WORD

All sit and extinguish tapers.

PSALM 1   "Psalm 141: Let My Prayer Rise Up," basics CD/CS1-#12, music book #25.
Assistant minister may incense Lectionary and assembly.

PSALM PRAYER   *All stand.*

God of all creation,
we praise you at the ending of this day.
Hear our prayers as we lift our hearts and voices to you.
May they rise like incense before you.

We pray through Christ our Lord. R/.

All sit.

PSALM 2   "Psalm 135: We Praise You," basics CD/CS1-#8, music book #21.

PSALM PRAYER   *All stand.*

God who is good,
may we praise the name of the Lord.
May we open our hearts to be mentors
to all who call upon your name.

You are Lord for ever and ever. R/.

All sit.

READING	Ephesians 3:14–21, *Lectionary #476*, Year II *or a reading appropriate to the liturgical season.* *Observe an extended period of silence after the reading at this service.*
GOSPEL CANTICLE	"Canticle of the Turning," basics CD/CS2-#13, music book #38. *All stand and sign themselves as they begin to sing the canticle. The assistant may incense the worship space.*

INTERCESSIONS

Or: *Book of Blessings*, p. 245–246

Presider:
We come together at the end of this day
bringing our prayers and needs before God.

Intercessor:
For leaders of the Church throughout the world and here in our city: that their openness to the Holy Spirit be a mark of their leadership, let us pray to the Lord: R/.

For the nations of the world that do not experience freedom and prosperity: that their struggles not be in vain, let us pray to the Lord: R/.

For children and young people all over our city and throughout the country: that they experience a safe and nurturing environment as they grow, let us pray to the Lord: R/.

For young people: that they may grow in faith and achieve their dreams, let us pray to the Lord: R/.

For members of our families who have died: that God give them eternal peace, let us pray to the Lord: R/.

Presider:
Loving God,
you know of our struggles
to be good parents and role models for our own children.
Help us to make right decisions guided by love.
Hear our prayers that we have placed before you.

We ask all of these things in the name of your Son, Jesus. R/.

THE LORD'S PRAYER

CONCLUDING PRAYER *Book of Blessings*, p. 241, B

BLESSING
Or: "Blessing," basics
CD/CS2-#16,
music book #41.

The Lord bless us and keep us!
The Lord let his face shine upon us and be gracious to us!
The Lord look upon us kindly and give us his peace! R/.

PREPARATION FOR EVENING PRAYER

GIVE THE GIFT OF PRAISE

DATE: **TIME:**

LOCATION:

OVERALL THEME   Praise of God at nightfall.

SCRIPTURE USED   Ephesians 3:14–21

SHORT REFLECTION   This liturgy is intended for use by parents groups, parish groups, or high school groups who meet in the evening. In "The Summons" we reflect upon our call to service, the psalms and incense lead us to praise, and in the reading from Scripture we celebrate the fullness of God. In the canticle, we turn to Mary in praise, and in the intercessions and Lord's Prayer we unite with the prayers of the world. Evening prayer is a simple prayer form, one that should become as familiar to us as the eucharistic liturgy.

QUESTIONS FOR STUDENTS TO PONDER
1. What is the fullness of God's presence in your life?
2. Who in your family shares God's mercy and love?
3. With whom can you share the glory of God?

CLOSING COMMENTS   Evening prayer provides an appropriate format for gathering in prayer and song at the close of the day. With the simple rhythm of psalms, responses, and readings, it provides a context for offering praise and thanks to God for the day or the gathering that is to follow. We call upon the presence of God to be with us in this hour, in this space, with this group, knowing that we are, by the nature of our prayer, connecting to the larger Church as well.

Any questions, please contact _____.

EUCHARISTIC CELEBRATION OF THE FEAST OF ALL SAINTS

NOVEMBER 1

PREPARATION

GETTING STARTED

Holy days of obligation are observed in a number of ways in a parish or a school setting. It is up to the individual community to determine how these feasts will be celebrated. For most young people, some catechesis about the place of these days in the life of the Church's liturgy is in order. This might take place in the context of religious education classes or may be part of the liturgy itself. This feast needs to be approached in a way that young people can see a connection with their own lives in the lives of the saints. The emphasis might best be placed on the call to holiness of all baptized persons. We need to remind them that holiness is not out of their reach, but rather, put simply, it is doing the ordinary in an extraordinary way. In each parish or school, this might be an opportunity to talk about the saint for whom the institution is named or a saint affiliated with the sponsoring religious congregation. Having reintroduced these figures important to the local community, it might be good to then focus on those individuals who are closer to the twentieth century—Frances Cabrini, Elizabeth Seton, Martin de Porres, and unofficially, John XXIII, Dorothy Day, and Mother Theresa.

MINISTERS

Student readers need to be selected and rehearsed in advance to proclaim the saints in the introductory rites.

ENVIRONMENT

Because this liturgy has as its focus our ancestors in our faith tradition, if there are any images of saints significant in this community, they should be displayed in a prominent place. If that is not possible, perhaps flowers or plants can be set in place. Who is the assembly for this liturgy? Is this a parish Mass? A small group that will be celebrating in the chapel? Will the whole school or parish be assembling? Depending on the space used, it should be appropriate for the celebration of Mass. Perhaps the names of the saints mentioned could be placed around the space in some way.

MUSIC

This feast is alive with images of following, answering a call, responsibility in faith—and the music selections should reflect these images.

The music selections for this celebration offer the opportunity to celebrate the introductory rites in a musically unified manner, a connected breath. It will demand some coordination with the presider, perhaps a run-through with the musicians. The rhythmic accompaniment suggests including Caribbean, Native

American, or African percussion instruments, perhaps even in a grand procession.

LITURGY CHECKLIST

❑ Copies of readings, given to readers in advance

❑ Copy of intercessions, given to intercessor in advance

❑ Copies of saint "introductions," given to speakers in advance

❑ Name signs or images of saints, in place

❑ Vestments for presider

❑ Lectionary, marked and in place

❑ Sacramentary, marked and in place

❑ Processional cross in place

❑ Candles, in place and lit

❑ Banners and banner stands in place

❑ Bowl of water and aspergill, in place

❑ Bread, wine, water, ciboria and communion cups, corporal, purificator(s), finger bowl, finger towel

❑ Incense pot, incense resins (in incense boat?), charcoal (lit)

❑ Worship aids distributed

❑ All involved in the procession are in place—any musicians, lector, intercessor, banner bearers, any assistants, presider

Other:

ORDER OF WORSHIP

INTRODUCTORY RITES

GATHERING SONG   "He Came Down" basics CD/CS1-#2, music book #15.

GREETING   *After the greeting by the presider, each "saint" would come forward and say his or her part:*

Presider: **We gather this day to remember those who are holy.**
We also remember those who have shown us ways to Christ.

Reader 1:   **Dorothy Day, who called the church to acts of peace and justice by ministering to the poor and homeless.**

Reader 2:   **Francis of Assisi, who left a comfortable life in a rich family to reach out to those who were the outcasts of society.**

Reader 3:   **Elizabeth Seton, mother, wife and religious, who made education a priority.**

Reader: 4   **Mother Theresa, who gave her entire life to giving dignity to the throwaway people in India and the rest of the world.**

Continue with saints meaningful to the community, possibly even including a much loved and admired member who recently died: someone's grandparent, parent, staff member, etc.

SPRINKLING RITE   *Sacramentary,* p. 358 (404), A
"We Are Marching (Siyahumba)," basics CD/CS1-#2, music book #15.

GLORY TO GOD   "Glory to God," basics CD/CS1-#3, music book #16.

OPENING PRAYER   **Let us pray.**
Or: *Sacramentary,*
p. 728 (660),   **God of power,**
alternative choice   **throughout history**
you have given us countless men and women of faith
whose works and lives inspire us today.
Let these people serve as a reminder to all of us
that we share in this call to holiness.
Strengthen us with your grace and courage
to be people who also make a difference
in the lives of others.

We ask this through our Lord Jesus Christ, your Son,
who lives and reigns with you and the Holy Spirit,
one God, for ever and ever. R/.

Reprise refrain of "He Came Down" basics CD/CS1-#2, music book #15.

LITURGY OF THE WORD

READING 1 Revelation 7:2–4, 9–14, *Lectionary #667*
Always observe some silence after the reading.

PSALM "Let Us Go Rejoicing (Psalm 122)," songs CD/CS-#12, music book #12.
Observe some silence after the psalm.

READING 2 1 John 3:1–3, *Lectionary #667*
Always observe some silence after the reading.

GOSPEL ACCLAMATION "Word of Truth and Life," basics CD/CS2-#6, music book #31.
You may wish to incense the gospel. See the appendix for suggestions.

GOSPEL Matthew 5:1–12, *Lectionary #667*

HOMILY/ REFLECTION NOTES *Before preparing the homily, you might want to ask yourself these questions:*
In your own faith growth and development, who are the saints that have inspired you?
What does it mean to be holy? Who are the holy people in your life?
Whom do you know or have you known who are living examples of the Beatitudes?
How can young people connect with the idea of holiness, saintliness?

GENERAL INTERCESSIONS Or: "Prayer of the Faithful," basics CD/CS2-#10, music book #35.
Be sure to add any intentions that are pertinent to your community. The intercessor should be in place before the presider gives the invitation to pray. These prayers may be led from the ambo.

Presider: **God of goodness,
who inspires ordinary people to do extraordinary things,
we bring our needs
and those of the people we love.
Hear our prayers.**

Intercessor: **For all those who stand up for the voiceless in our society; for those who protect children, the poor, the elderly: that they receive strength to continue their heroic work, let us pray to the Lord: R/.**

For parents and grandparents who give unselfishly of time, talents, and self to the next generation, let us pray to the Lord: R/.

For those who work on the sidelines, who may never receive a lot of notice, but who do all their ordinary tasks in an extraordinary way, let us pray to the Lord: R/.

For those who live with illness or disability on a daily basis: that their suffering not go unnoticed in this world or the next, let us pray to the Lord: R/.

Other intentions may be added here.

For all those who have gone before us in faith: that they experience lasting joy and peace in God's presence, let us pray to the Lord: R/.

The intercessor should face the presider and not leave until the prayer is finished.

Presider: **Father,**
hear the prayers from the hearts of your people,
given voice in the name of Jesus, your Son. R/.

LITURGY OF THE EUCHARIST

PREPARATION OF THE ALTAR AND THE GIFTS
"Come and Follow Me," songs CD/CS-#3, music book #3.

PRAYER OVER THE GIFTS
Or: *Sacramentary,* p. 728 (660)
God, giver of all gifts,
accept our offerings,
these simple gifts of bread and wine
that represent our lives
and all that we offer to you.
Bless the work of our hands.

We ask this through Christ our Lord. R/.

EUCHARISTIC PRAYER
Sacramentary, proper preface p. 515 (488), sung preface p. 514 (1007); p. 542 (562), Eucharistic Prayer I
"Eucharistic Acclamations," basics CD/CS2-#11, music book #36.

COMMUNION RITE

LORD'S PRAYER

SIGN OF PEACE

BREAKING OF THE BREAD
"Lamb of God," basics CD/CS2-#12, music book #37.
Ask the other ministers to help break bread and pour wine so this rite will not be extended.

COMMUNION SONG
"You Are Mine," songs CD/CS-#9, music book #9.
Always observe some silence after Communion.

**PRAYER AFTER
COMMUNION**
Or : *Sacramentary,*
p. 729 (661)

God of all history,
we know that it is not always easy to be extraordinary
or to live by our convictions.
We need you
and the support of those who love us
to be the saints that we are called to be.

We ask this through Christ our Lord. R/.

CONCLUDING RITE

**GREETING AND
BLESSING**
Or: *Sacramentary,*
p. 577 (535), #18,
All Saints

"Blessing," basics CD/CS2-#16, music book #41.

DISMISSAL

RECESSIONAL SONG

"Joyfully Singing," songs CD/CS-#8, music book #8.

PREPARATION FOR EUCHARISTIC CELEBRATION OF THE FEAST OF ALL SAINTS

GIVE THE GIFT OF HOLINESS

DATE: **TIME:**

LOCATION:

OVERALL THEME — Living out the call to holiness.

SCRIPTURE USED — Revelation 7:2–4; 9–14 / 1 John 3:1–3 / Matthew 5:1–12

SHORT REFLECTION — The concepts of sainthood and holiness may seem out of reach and antiquated to young people. The tradition of studying the lives of the saints has most likely not been a part of their experience, coming in contact with the idea only when selecting a confirmation name and the research that may result. Oftentimes, the stories of saints contain information about their lives that may actually seem strange or weird to most people today. In discussing this, it would be helpful to get past the idiosyncrasies of these people and get at their holiness and greatness in light of any era or time period. A discussion of more contemporary models might be helpful—Dorothy Day, Mother Theresa, etc. If you ask them about whom they think are saints, spend some time exploring the characteristics and qualities that they identify. The questions below might help.

QUESTIONS FOR STUDENTS TO PONDER
1. What does it mean to be holy?
2. Who, in your understanding, would you consider to be a holy person?
3. What qualities might you connect with a saintly person?
4. Is sainthood possible for you? Why? Why not?
5. How can we, today, in the twentieth century, live out the words of the Beatitudes in today's gospel reading?
6. What help do you need to be a "saint"?

CLOSING COMMENTS — Though young people certainly may need help in identifying their own call to holiness, they are more apt to notice these characteristics in others. They often identify their grandparents as holy people. Whether discussing people in their own lives or those who more publicly make a statement, it is important to emphasize that though not all of us may have our names included in a litany, the holiness to which we are called is not beyond our reach.

Any questions, please contact _____.

EUCHARISTIC CELEBRATION
IN THE FACE OF DEATH

NOVEMBER, ALL SOULS
or anytime there has been a death in the community

PREPARATION

GETTING STARTED

Death is difficult whenever it happens. Many young people in high school may be facing it for the first time when grandparents die. Some, unfortunately, have already had to deal with the untimely death of a parent or a sibling, either before starting high school or during those four years. Certainly in those instances, they reach out and receive support from friends and, in a more formal way, from the school community. However, there are very few school or parish communities that have been untouched by the death of a young person; it is always tragic and often sudden. This would also apply to the death of a teacher or a staff member who had contact with the students. Certainly, schools and communities have crisis plans in place in the event that this does happen in order to deal with the feelings of grief and helplessness. In addition, as a faith community, there also needs to be a response that helps teens to focus on the Christian message of hope in the Resurrection. Because many teens are at a stage in their own faith development of questioning and uncertainty, the death of a friend or member of the school community may further compound ambiguous feelings about God and faith. It is important that at a time like this the focus is not on trying to answer the question of why God did this but rather that, in this tragedy, how young people can look to God and their faith for strength in this difficult time. The sprinkling rite is included in this liturgy to assist in making a strong connection to baptism, just as that same connection is integral to the funeral liturgy.

The prayers and readings focus on the hope given to us by Jesus in his own victory over death. Depending on the circumstances of the death, adjustments may need to be made in the prayers or readings; the Order of Christian Funerals would provide additional prayers, commentaries, and readings that might be more appropriate. As it is written the liturgy may be used as a memorial service; however, with some adjustments it could be used simply during the month of November as a way to remember all the deceased in the lives of the community members.

If the service is a memorial for an individual (or individuals), consider having someone eulogize the deceased before the opening song. If there is a song associated with the deceased, this would be an appropriate time to include it. After the remembrances and a moment of silence, the cantor could then invite the assembly to stand and join in the opening song.

MINISTERS

Though it is important to acknowledge those who may have been related to or friends with the deceased by inviting their involvement in the liturgy, it is also important to utilize students and other members of the community who are comfortable in these roles. Cross and candles should be part of the procession along with the lector with Lectionary, the student who leads intercessions, as well as the bowl of water and aspergill for the sprinkling rite; however, the water and aspergill may already be in place on a table near the altar. If the celebrant is not known to the majority of the community, he should be given the necessary information about the deceased and be introduced to the assembly. Choose Communion ministers as needed, maintaining balance between involving the appropriate students and the liturgical roles.

ENVIRONMENT

Is this celebration going to involve the entire community? Will this liturgy be celebrated in a smaller space—a chapel, an all-purpose room? The use of white vestments and any accompanying linens should reflect the resurrection nature of the liturgy. The purchase of flowers is appropriate to enhance the space. Perhaps, if it is a member of the community who has died, a green plant or some perennial could later be planted outside as a permanent symbol of the life of this person. At many wakes, it is becoming more common to see picture collages of the deceased. Whether or not something like this is used as part of the environment would be a judgment call in the community. Do not display these items on the altar itself; consider placing them on a suitable table next to the ambo. A paschal candle, if available, would also be appropriate.

MUSIC

The music for this service serves as praise of God, as well as a comfort to those who morn. By "eulogizing" before the liturgy proper, the living are allowed to move from sadness to joy. Music selections are chosen accordingly.

"You Are Mine" is filled with images of hope. Psalm 23 contains a traditional image of the passing from death to life. "With the Lord" recalls God's mercy. The Communion song calls us to move from our personal grief into world lamentation. The psalm at the conclusion is one that is often used as a vision of the New Jerusalem, and thus our celebration of eternal life.

LITURGY CHECKLIST

- ❑ Copies of readings, given to readers in advance
- ❑ Copy of intercessions, given to intercessor in advance
- ❑ Any memorial, collages (if used) in place
- ❑ Vestments for presider
- ❑ Lectionary, marked and in place
- ❑ Sacramentary, marked and in place
- ❑ Processional cross in place
- ❑ Candles (including paschal candle?), in place and lit
- ❑ Banners and banner stands in place
- ❑ Bowl of water and aspergill in place
- ❑ Bread, wine, water, ciboria and communion cups, corporal, purificator(s), finger bowl, finger towel

❑ Incense pot, incense resins (in incense boat?), charcoal (lit)

❑ Worship aids distributed

❑ All involved in the procession are in place—lector, intercessor, any assistants, presider

Other:

ORDER OF WORSHIP

INTRODUCTORY RITES

The service may be preceded by a eulogy of the deceased and memorial music, poems, readings, etc. After a pause for a moment of silence, the cantor should invite the assembly to rise and join in the opening song.

GATHERING SONG   "You Are Mine," songs CD/CS-#9, music book #9.

GREETING

PENITENTIAL RITE   Lord Jesus, you call us to live in the light of life:
Lord, have mercy. R/.

Christ Jesus, you promise us eternal life if we follow your ways:
Christ, have mercy. R/.

Lord Jesus, you are hope in the darkness of death:
Lord, have mercy. R/.

May almighty God . . .

OPENING PRAYER
Or: Sacramentary,
p. 961 (870), #3 A For
One Person, alternative

Let us pray.

God of all hope,
we ask you to give us strength and support
as we gather in memory of _____.
We pray,
confident that he (she) is at peace with you,
celebrating in the victory over death with your Son, Jesus.

Who lives and reigns with you the Holy Spirit,
one God, for ever and ever. R/.

LITURGY OF THE WORD

READING 1   Romans 8:31–35, 37–39, *Lectionary #790-6*
Always observe some silence after the reading.

PSALM   "Psalm 23: Shepherd Me, O God," basics CD/CS1-#10, music book #23.
Observe some silence after the psalm.

GOSPEL ACCLAMATION   "Word of Truth and Life," basics CD/CS2-#6, music book #31.
During Lent: "Open Our Ears," basics CD/CS2-#5, music book #30.
You may wish to incense the gospel. See the appendix for suggestions.

GOSPEL   Luke 7:11–17, *Lectionary #793-6*

HOMILY/ REFLECTION NOTES: *As you prepare your homily, you may want to consider the following questions:*

When have you had questions about the mystery of life and death?
How have you dealt with those times in your own life when you have felt helpless in the face of situations beyond your control?
In what ways have you found comfort in faith in difficult times?
What images, ideas, words offer you hope?

GENERAL INTERCESSIONS   Or: "Prayer of the Faithful," basics CD/CS2-#10, music book #35.
Be sure to add any intentions that are pertinent to your community. The intercessor should be in place before the presider gives the invitation to pray. These prayers may be led from the ambo.

Presider: **Compassionate God,**
in this time of sadness
we come to you with our needs and hopes.
Hear us in this difficult time.

Intercessor: **For the family of _____: that they be given the hope they will see their loved one again, let us pray to the Lord: R/.**

For the friends and all those whose lives were touched by _____: that their faith be a support to them, let us pray to the Lord: R/.

For all in our community who in the past year have experienced the death of someone they love; that they be given strength in your promise of eternal life, let us pray to the Lord: R/.

Other intentions may be added here.

For those who are seriously ill and facing death, let us pray to the Lord: R/.

The intercessor should face the presider and not leave until the prayer is finished.

Presider: **Loving God,**
even in this difficult time,
we trust that you hear our prayers,
for we make them in the name of Jesus the Lord. R/.

LITURGY OF THE EUCHARIST

PREPARATION OF THE ALTAR AND THE GIFTS

"With the Lord," songs CD/CS-#7, music book #7.

PRAYER OVER THE GIFTS
Or: *Sacramentary,*
p. 961 (870), #3 A,
For One Person

God of tears and laughter,
we come to you with heavy hearts as we offer these gifts.
We remember _____ with love,
believing that she (he) lives with you.

Grant this through Christ our Lord. R/.

EUCHARISTIC PRAYER

Sacramentary, p. 556 (517), Eucharistic Prayer IV
Or: preface for Christian Death, IV, sung p. 532 (1017), or p. 533 (497); or V,
    sung p. 534 (1018), or p. 535 (498); and p. 552 (513), Eucharistic Prayer III
"Eucharistic Acclamations," basics CD/CS2-#11, music book #36.

COMMUNION RITE

LORD'S PRAYER

SIGN OF PEACE

BREAKING OF THE BREAD

"Lamb of God," basics CD/CS2-#12, music book #37.
Ask the other ministers to help break bread and pour wine so this rite will not be extended.

COMMUNION SONG

"For Living, for Dying," songs CD/CS-#5, music book #5.
Always observe some silence after Communion.

PRAYER AFTER COMMUNION
Or: *Sacramentary,*
p. 961 (870), A, For
One Person

Let us pray.

Gentle God,
we take hope and strength
from this holy meal we have shared.
May our friend _____,
who once shared this meal with us,
find never-ending peace with you and your Son, Jesus,
who lives and reigns with you for ever and ever. R/.

CONCLUDING RITE

GREETING AND
BLESSING

"Blessing," basics CD/CS2-#16, music book #41.

Or: *Sacramentary*, p. 731 (663), Solemn Blessing or Prayer over the People, All Souls

Or: p. 578 (536), Solemn Blessing, #20, The Dead

DISMISSAL

RECESSIONAL SONG

"Let Us Go Rejoicing (Psalm 122)," songs CD/CS-#12, music book #12.

PREPARATION FOR EUCHARISTIC CELEBRATION IN THE FACE OF DEATH

GIVE THE GIFT OF HOPE

DATE: **TIME:**

LOCATION:

OVERALL THEME   We look to God in our times of doubt and struggle.

SCRIPTURE USED   Romans 8:31–35, 37–39 / Luke 7:11–17

SHORT REFLECTION   Just as adolescence is a time of struggle and growth toward independence on so many levels, it is common for young people to question issues of faith and the norms of established religion with which they have grown up. There is no more heartfelt and anguished question for them as Why when they deal with death or any serious loss. They are quick to ask, If God indeed is so good and loving, why did he take my mother, friend, grandfather, etc. Harold Kushner, in his classic book *When Bad Things Happen to Good People*, raised the same questions. And just as Kushner had to change his mindset in regard to how he viewed God, we need to gently listen and perhaps nudge teens not to dwell on the question, but rather on how they will respond to the situation. They need to be reminded that they are not alone in their sadness—that God stands with them in their grief. They need to be reminded of the whole focus of the Christian faith, which is Resurrection-centered; that in dying, Jesus won victory over death, a victory in which we share because of our baptism.

QUESTIONS FOR STUDENTS TO PONDER
1. Where do you look for hope in the difficult times in your life?
2. How does nature in its life-death-life cycle provide comfort and connection with the Christian message?
3. What word(s) or saying from Scripture can give you hope when you face the death of someone you love?
4. Every time we say the Creed we profess our belief in the communion of saints. How can that be a source of comfort?
5. What are the happy memories you have of this person that will keep them alive for you?

CLOSING COMMENTS   Teens may respond to a death situation in either of two ways in regard to their faith. On the one hand, they may blame God for this loss and turn away from any connection to Church and prayer. On the other hand, they may find genuine comfort in the faith of their family and community and pray with deeper conviction. We need to be sensitive to the fact that the students in our presence may be at either of these two ends of the spectrum or just about anywhere in between.

Any questions, please contact _____.

EUCHARISTIC CELEBRATION OF THANKSGIVING

NOVEMBER

PREPARATION

For many of us, Thanksgiving Day signifies the beginning of the winter holiday season and may also provide the first long weekend break. For young people it could also mean seeing friends who are on their first trip home from college. For just about everyone, it includes a celebration of food and family get-togethers. But like many of the celebrations in our society today, the deeper, spiritual dimension has often been lost or given secondary status. Gratitude for an abundant harvest is also not part of the experience of most people today. Observing the upcoming Thanksgiving holiday in the context of the Eucharist provides young people with an opportunity to focus on giving gratitude to God for abundance given in all aspects of their lives. This celebration also provides a chance to strike that balance between being thankful for all that we have and responding to those who are in need. During this time of year, many local, national, and international organizations observe fast days aligned with food drives. Schools and churches might choose to select one of these during the time before Thanksgiving. Whatever route is chosen, taking up a food collection as part of this liturgy is a powerful testimony to giving from our abundance. Depending on the size of the school or group, this food drive may be ongoing in the week before the liturgy, and class or homeroom representatives can bring the collected food to the Mass. If it is well publicized, students will come to the liturgy with their food offering and individually present it during the presentation of gifts. In any case, there needs to be a space designated for the placement of the food so as not to obscure the altar or obstruct access to the sanctuary. Directions for presenting the food offerings should include how to approach the altar, where to put the offering, and how to return to their seats.

MINISTERS

For this liturgy, assistants carrying the processional cross and candles should be part of the entrance procession along with the students who will read from Scripture and the reader of the intercessions. These students or others could be utilized to help with the food offerings during the presentation of gifts. There may be a need for some directing and ushering depending on the size of the group. Oftentimes, students may forget their food offering; one of the ministers could place a basket for monetary offerings if any of the students should choose to make one.

There should be sufficient students designated to assist with Communion distribution—both cup and bread. Though the concept of gratitude is a universal one, if there is a member of the community who is willing to speak to this, he or she may be invited to do so instead of the presider, especially if he is not part of the community.

ENVIRONMENT

Since this celebration occurs in mid autumn, it would enhance the worship space to use the colors of the season—yellows, reds, gold, and orange. This may include the purchase of fresh flowers or the placement of a silk arrangement. The use of symbols of harvest—sheaves of wheat, grapes, cornucopia—would also make attractive and appropriate additions to the space. If the group is small, baskets might be used as collection containers for food offerings. Even food donated earlier might be left in baskets at the foot of the altar.

MUSIC

Music during this liturgy should reflect how the community is already praying. Student musicians by now are in fine form, so use them. (The recording for this project was done by a "pop" choir of a local Catholic high school).

Be prepared that the preparation of the gifts may last longer than usual, especially if the assembly comes forward with their offerings. The Taizé chant "O Lord, Hear Our Prayer" offers many options: layer instruments, hum instead of sing, layer parts, sing a cappella. Continue to weave this music throughout the rite to the conclusion of the prayer over the gifts.

The concluding song is wonderful for dismissal. During the third verse have the assembly begin to move out of their places, allowing the ending refrain to repeat as long as necessary. A strong cantor can "scat" over the final refrain. Look to local jazz singers who may be able to coach your cantors.

LITURGY CHECKLIST

- ❏ Copies of readings, given to readers in advance
- ❏ Copy of intercessions, given to intercessor in advance
- ❏ Baskets as needed, in place
- ❏ Ushers rehearsed
- ❏ Vestments for presider
- ❏ Lectionary, marked and in place
- ❏ Sacramentary, marked and in place
- ❏ Processional cross in place
- ❏ Candles, in place and lit
- ❏ Bread, wine, water, ciboria and communion cups, corporal, purificator(s), finger bowl, finger towel
- ❏ Incense pot, incense resins (in incense boat?), charcoal (lit)
- ❏ Worship aids distributed
- ❏ All involved in the procession are in place—lector, intercessor, any assistants, presider

Other:

ORDER OF WORSHIP

INTRODUCTORY RITES

GATHERING SONG | "Come, All You People," basics CD/CS2-#1, music book #26.

GREETING

PENITENTIAL RITE
Or: *Sacramentary,*
p. 361 *(406)*, invitation C
with form C-ii *(c-2)*

Jesus, you taught us by word and example to give freely to those
    in need.
Lord, have mercy. R/.

Jesus, you gave your own life so that we might live forever.
Christ, have mercy. R/.

Jesus, we sometimes take all that we have for granted.
Lord, have mercy. R/.

May almighty God have mercy on us,
forgive us our sins,
and bring us to everlasting life. R/.

OPENING PRAYER
Or: *Sacramentary,* p. 923
(843), #39-B,
In Thanksgiving

Let us pray.

Generous God,
in your goodness and wisdom,
you have given us your many gifts of creation that bring us joy.
We thank you for the changing seasons
and the many plants and animals that provide us with food.
We are grateful, too,
for those who do you your work on this earth—
those who love us and care for us.
Help us to love them and you with grateful hearts.

We ask this through our Lord Jesus Christ, your Son,
who lives and reigns with you and the Holy Spirit,
one God, for ever and ever. R/.

LITURGY OF THE WORD

READING 1 | Colossians 3:12–17, *Lectionary #882-3*
Always observe some silence after the reading.

PSALM "Psalm 80: Lord, Let Us See Your Kindness," basics CD/CS1-#4, music book #17.
Observe some silence after the psalm.

GOSPEL ACCLAMATION "Word of Truth and Life," basics CD/CS2-#6, music book #31.
You may wish to incense the gospel. See the appendix for suggestions.

GOSPEL Luke 17:11–19, *Lectionary #885-2*

HOMILY/
REFLECTION NOTES

As you prepare your homily, you may want to consider the following questions:

What are some times in your life when you were truly grateful for something or someone? How did you express that gratitude?

How did it feel when something you had done or given someone went unnoticed?

Identify situations in which you have taken something or someone for granted.

Reflect on the popularity of books like *Simple Abundance* and its accompanying *Gratitude Journal*.

Would you have been the one cured leper to return and offer thanks? Why? Why not?

GENERAL
INTERCESSIONS
Or: "Prayer of the Faithful,"
basics CD/CS2-#10,
music book #35.

Begin an instrumental version of "O Lord, Hear Our Prayer," basics CD/CS2-#8, music book #33, continuing through to conclusion of the prayer over the gifts.
Be sure to add any intentions that are pertinent to your community. The intercessor should be in place before the presider gives the invitation to pray. These prayers may be led from the ambo.

Presider: **Loving Creator,
you have already been so generous to us.
We ask you now to hear our prayers
for those in special need of your love and gifts.**

Intercessor: **For leaders in our school, our community and our Church who give unselfishly of their time and energies, let us pray to the Lord: R/.**

For those who labor as farmers and those who care for the land: that they be blessed with a good harvest, let us pray to the Lord: R/.

For those who minister to the homeless, to the hungry, to those in shelters, to the sick: that they be given strength to continue their work, let us pray to the Lord: R/.

For our parents and other family members who are generous with their time so that we may have the things we need, let us to the Lord: R/.

For all of us: that we may be inspired with unselfishness and generosity of heart to respond to the needs of those around us, let us pray to the Lord: R/.

Other intentions may be added here.

For those who have died, let us pray to the Lord: R/.

The intercessor should face the presider and not leave until the prayer is finished.

Presider: **Giver of gifts,
hear us and be generous to us
We ask this in the name of Jesus. R/.**

LITURGY OF THE EUCHARIST

PREPARATION OF THE ALTAR AND THE GIFTS

*Along with the gifts of bread and wine, food offerings will be presented.
"O Lord, Hear Our Prayer," basics CD/CS2-#8, music book #33 continues,
including sung portions. Last repeat might be quietly hummed or instrumental so that
it may continue through to the conclusion of the prayer over the gifts.*

PRAYER OVER THE GIFTS:
Or: *Sacramentary,*
p. 923 (843), #39-B,
In Thanksgiving

**Loving God,
we offer you our gifts of bread and wine.
We bring offerings of food as well,
a sign of our thankfulness for all that you have given to us.
Help us to be grateful for what we have
and generous with our abundance.**

We ask this through Christ our Lord R/.

EUCHARISTIC PRAYER

Sacramentary, proper preface of Thanksgiving Day, p. 541 (501), sung preface
p. 540 (1022); p. 552 (511), Eucharistic Prayer III.
"Eucharistic Acclamations," basics CD/CS2-#11, music book #36.

COMMUNION RITE

LORD'S PRAYER

SIGN OF PEACE

BREAKING OF THE BREAD

"Lamb of God," basics CD/CS2-#12, music book #37.
Ask the other ministers to help break bread and pour wine so this rite will not be extended.

COMMUNION SONG

"Psalm 34: Taste and See," basics CD/CS1-#7, music book #20.
Always observe some silence after Communion.

PRAYER AFTER COMMUNION
Or: *Sacramentary*,
p. 923 (843), #39-B,
In Thanksgiving

Let us pray.

God of all times and seasons,
you taught us what it means to give and not count the cost,
by giving us your own Son, Jesus.
In this season of being thankful,
remind us to be willing to give from the wealth of what we have.
Help us not to take the people and things in our lives for granted.

We ask this through Christ our Lord. R/.

CONCLUDING RITE

GREETING AND BLESSING
Or: "Blessing," basics CD/CS2-#16, music book #41.
Sacramentary, p. 574 (533), #12, Ordinary Time III, or #14, Ordinary Time V

DISMISSAL

RECESSIONAL SONG
"Joyfully Singing," songs CD/CS-#8, music book #8.

PREPARATION FOR A EUCHARISTIC CELEBRATION OF THANKSGIVING

GIVE THE GIFT OF SINCERE THANKSGIVING

DATE: **TIME:**

LOCATION:

OVERALL THEME   Being thankful for all that we have—responding with generosity.

SCRIPTURE USED   Colossians 3:12–17 / Luke 17:11–19

SHORT REFLECTION   Young people are on the receiving end of much in their lives simply because of financial dependence. They may often rely on parents and older siblings for transportation. If they are not working, they are dependent on others for spending money or help in purchasing what they need. They may often see themselves as having "less" than what their classmates have and, driven by our consumer society, always want more. Thanksgiving offers them a chance to reflect on all the gifts they already possess, from the very simple ones to the generosity of parents and others in their lives. It is easy for teens to take this real abundance for granted. The gospel reading helps them to focus on the importance of gratitude and giving voice to the thanks that often goes unsaid. It also asks them to focus on those in our world that do not possess as much in the way of food, shelter, and clothing. As followers of Jesus, it is our responsibility to respond to those needs. This would be an appropriate time to discuss the food drive and remind students to bring food offerings for the liturgy.

QUESTIONS FOR STUDENTS TO PONDER
1. Make a list of the things in your life for which you are most grateful.
2. Who are the people in your life who need to hear the words "thank you" more frequently?
3. Would you be the person to return to Jesus to thank him for being cured? Why or why not?
4. How can you share your abundance with others in specific, concrete ways?

CLOSING COMMENTS   As we discuss all that we have for which we are grateful, recognize, too, that some of your own students may be in the position of receiving assistance from others. It is important to emphasize not only the material abundance for which we are grateful, but also those intangibles, like health, sense of humor, friendship, good weather, etc. Even though we have not all been equally blessed, we can all find something for which to be thankful. Students may want to start their own "gratitude journal."

Any questions, please contact _____.

ADVENT RECONCILIATION SERVICE
DECEMBER

PREPARATION

GETTING STARTED

The season of Advent might begin rather inauspiciously for many students because it usually follows or brings to a close the Thanksgiving break. Because of its position in the calendar, this makes it hard to anticipate or prepare for, since the Thanksgiving service and holiday immediately precede it. Inevitably, the season is cut short in school life because the Christmas recess may begin before the fourth Sunday of Advent. Though the liturgical life of the Church highlights and focuses on the four Sundays that precede the celebration of Christmas, this rhythm and significance get lost in the school setting or even youth group meetings. In order for Advent to retain its richness and prominence in the Church year, it is important in schools and youth groups to make the remaining days of the season as significant as possible. One of the ways in which to do this on a school- or parishwide basis is to focus on reconciliation in a prayer experience using the themes of Advent. One would hope that within the school community there is an Advent wreath in a common area, and that teachers within the school are observing Advent in some way. The readings here were chosen from among the Sunday texts. Depending upon when in Advent this service is celebrated, other choices from the Lectionary might be more appropriate. It is important to focus on this time as one of preparation—not just for Christmas but for the coming of Jesus at the end of time as well. With that as a focus, the ideas of reconciliation and change of heart take on a deeper significance. Stress levels of teachers, youth leaders, and students take a giant leap at this time of year, so this service can be a source of peace and centering amid the noise and busyness that surrounds us.

MINISTERS

If the community does not have a resident priest or chaplain, the service could be led by the campus minister or other appropriate member of the community. The person who serves as presider may reflect on the Scriptures, although it wouldn't have to be the same person. If perhaps students are enrolled in a ministry course or taking a class focused on prayer and liturgy, sharing a reflection would be an appropriate outcome of the class. Student readers for Scripture, the invocations, and intercessions need to be rehearsed. Perhaps representatives from a variety of groups within the community could be invited to extinguish and relight the candles in the ritual that follows the Gospel—one representative from first through fourth years, one from faculty, one from administration would be one configuration.

ENVIRONMENT

If the service is not celebrated in a church or a chapel already enhanced with the symbols of Advent, the space used needs to reflect the season. The colors of purple or blue-violet should be used. The Advent wreath and its candles need to be large enough and positioned so that all can see them. Because the focus is on the movement from darkness to light, dim lighting throughout the worship space is necessary. In addition to the candles of the Advent wreath, six more candles need to be lit and placed around the focal area. These need to be accessible. The use of a Jesse tree may also enhance this service.

MUSIC

Music is integral to this service. Weaving music with the prayer will enhance the prayer so that the familiar refrain of "Rejoice, rejoice" rings throughout the season.

The gathering song may be the up-tempo version of "Come, O Come, Emmanuel" found on the project recording, or begin with a chant setting and move to the rhythmic setting. Instrumentalists may keep the music moving under the presider's greeting, with the assembly singing in response the refrain from "Come, O Come, Emmanuel."

The psalm suggested is found in the collection *Give Your Gifts*, but it is not a psalm "proper" to Advent. You may wish to check other resources, such as the David Haas setting of Psalm 25 found in *Walking by Faith* and melodically based on "Come, O Come, Emmanuel."

Careful coordination is needed for the ritual and general intercessions as presented here to successfully weave "Come, O Come Emmanuel / O Antiphons" with the spoken texts. At first it may look daunting, but it is very exciting when readers, musicians, and even movement people make this come together. Remember to keep it simple yet profound.

After each ritual statement and extinguishing of the candle, have the choir, cantor, or schola sing one of the O Antiphons.

Towards the end of the meditation period the musicians should start transitions back to "Come, O Come, Emmanuel." Underscore the general intercessions with music and then end the intercessions with the overlapping of the O Antiphons while the assembly sings the refrain of "Come, O Come, Emmanuel." It sounds involved, but it does work. Towards the end of this piece, you may wish to surround the assembly with movement people carrying lit candles.

The closing song harkens our minds back to the fact that it is Mary's yes that keeps us turning and moving.

LITURGY CHECKLIST

❑ Copies of readings, given to readers in advance
❑ Copy of intercessions, given to intercessor in advance
❑ Advent wreath and candles
❑ Candlesnuffer
❑ Alb for leader
❑ Lectionary, marked and in place
❑ Sacramentary, marked and in place

❑ Processional cross in place
❑ Six additional candles (in Advent colors or white), lit (two may be used in procession)
❑ Worship aids distributed
❑ All involved in the procession are in place—lector, intercessor, any assistants, presider

Other:

ORDER OF WORSHIP

INTRODUCTORY RITES

GATHERING SONG

"Come, O Come, Emmanuel / O Antiphons," basics CD/CS1-#1, music book #14.

GREETING

My friends,
today we come together (as we begin)
to celebrate the season of Advent.
We call upon Jesus, our brother,
who brings the light of hope and reconciliation
to the darkest corners of our lives.

The people who have walked in darkness
have seen a great light;
on those who dwell in deep shadow,
a light has shown.

All sing refrain "Rejoice, rejoice. . . ."

OPENING PRAYER
Book of Blessings,
p. 654, #1532

The presider or student representative lights the appropriate number of candles on the Advent wreath.

LITURGY OF THE WORD

READING 1

Isaiah 11:1–10, *Lectionary #4-A*
Always observe some silence after the reading.

PSALM

"Psalm 63: As Morning Breaks," basics CD/CS1-#6, music book #19.
Or: A setting of Psalm 25 or 85 familiar to the assembly.
Observe some silence after the psalm.

GOSPEL ACCLAMATION

"Word of Truth and Life," basics CD/CS2-#6, music book #31.

GOSPEL

Mark 1:1–8, *Lectionary #5*

HOMILY/
REFLECTION NOTES

What kind of "preparation" do the readings inspire in you?
How does the imagery in the first reading enhance your understanding of peace that was promised with the coming of Jesus?
How do you deal with the busyness at this time of year that might work against establishing a time of peace?
Where do you see the greatest need for reconciliation—in our world, our city, and our community?

Why is reconciliation so important in our interpersonal relationships?

RITUAL

The nature of this ritual is something like an examination of conscience. As the statement is read by the reader and responded to by the assembly, a community representative extinguishes one of the six additional candles while one of the O Antiphons is sung. This continues in the same way for each of the six statements.

When we speak words of violence instead of peace
O Antiphon.

When we make judgments about others based on their appearance
O Antiphon.

When we do not speak the truth
O Antiphon.

When we make choices that diminish rather than enhance life
O Antiphon.

When we put our faith in possessions and money rather than God
O Antiphon.

When we build walls instead of bridges
O Antiphon.

This should be followed by a brief moment of silence, inviting the assembly to reflect on the ways they have contributed to the darkness in our world.

GENERAL
INTERCESSIONS

Or: "Prayer of the Faithful," basics CD/CS2-#10, music book #35.

Presider:

God, creator of the stars that light our way in the night,
we ask you to hear our prayers
in this holy season of Advent
for all those who bring light into our world.
We need your help to wait patiently
for the coming of Jesus, your Son,
who is light.

As each petition is read and responded to, the same representative relights one of the candles.

Intercessor:

For parents and teachers, who share with us the light of wisdom and guidance as we find our way, let us pray to the Lord: R/.

For families and grandparents, who light our lives with unconditional love, let us pray to the Lord: R/.

For friends, who always know when we need light and laughter, let us pray to the Lord: R/.

For those in our community who so generously give of their time and talents so that others may experience the light of hope, let us pray to the Lord: R/.

For those among our loved ones who have died: that we one day may share with them the light of peace, let us pray to the Lord: R/.

Loving God,
we trust that you will always answer our prayers
because you have given us your Son, Jesus,
to be light and life for us.

We ask this in his name. R/.

LORD'S PRAYER   Let us join our hands and hearts in the words
that Jesus taught us to use when we pray: R/.

SIGN OF PEACE   Let us now offer to each other a sign of Advent peace and reconciliation.

CONCLUDING RITE

GREETING AND   God,
BLESSING   you know us
and how easily we lose our way.
We ask you to be with us in this holy season of Advent
and help us to be people who bring more light than darkness into
    this world.

We ask all of these things in the name of Jesus,
who is our light
and lives and reigns with you and the Holy Spirit,
one God, for ever and ever. R/.

BLESSING   "Blessing," basics CD/CS2-#16, music book #41.
Or: *Sacramentary*, p. 3 (79), Solemn Blessing for Advent

DISMISSAL

RECESSIONAL SONG   "Canticle of the Turning," basics CD/CS2-#13, music book #38.

PREPARATION FOR ADVENT RECONCILIATION SERVICE

GIVE THE GIFT OF FORGIVENESS

DATE: **TIME:**

LOCATION:

OVERALL THEME   Bringing light to a darkened world.

SCRIPTURE USED   Isaiah 11:1–10 / Mark 1:1–8

SHORT REFLECTION   Because this season so immediately follows Thanksgiving and school recesses before it is over, catechesis is necessary to emphasize its importance in the liturgical life of the Church. The preparation that John calls us to in his gospel is one of personal conversion, rather than Christmas shopping and decorating. This requires a shift in perspective for most young people. We would encourage them to view these weeks before Christmas as a time of quiet anticipation—one of readying our own selves for the coming of Jesus both at that time in history but also at the end of time. How are we to prepare? John speaks of reforming one's life. The reading from Isaiah talks about the kind of world that will exist when Jesus comes onto the scene. Since this peaceable kingdom is still a long way off, our personal preparation during this period might involve reflecting how we as individuals could become more a bringer of light and peace into the world, even if it is only the most proximate world in which we live in a day-to-day basis. As followers of Jesus, it is left to us to do our best to create a world that resembles the one Isaiah describes, and when we fail, we need to acknowledge those failures and try to do better next time. This service provides a spiritual oasis in an otherwise hectic and stressful time for students, faculty, and staff.

QUESTIONS FOR STUDENTS TO PONDER
1. What can I do in my personal life to "prepare" for the coming of Jesus?
2. How have I diminished the amount of light in the world?
3. What can I do specifically to bring more light into my immediate world?
4. What does "reform your lives" mean for me today in this age?
5. How can I bring peace into this sometimes very stressful time of year?

CLOSING COMMENTS   Advent speaks to us of a coming: Jesus coming into the world, light coming to a place of darkness, peace coming where it did not previously exist. Advent invites each one of us to look into our own hearts and examine how we can best prepare for this coming.

Any questions, please contact _____.

EUCHARISTIC CELEBRATION IN HONOR OF THE BLESSED VIRGIN MARY

DECEMBER 8 OR OTHER MARIAN FEAST

PREPARATION

GETTING STARTED

The feast of the Immaculate Conception often confuses young people—and many adults! It is often misunderstood as referring to Jesus' conception rather than Mary's. So though it is important to know that Mary, from the time she was conceived, was without sin, it is equally important to know that this certainly sets Mary aside as a very special person. But rather than focus on what happened to Mary as some passive observer in her own life, emphasize the actions Mary took on faith. Imagine a young girl who took the word of an angel or messenger of God and said yes because she trusted and believed in God. This was not the response of a passive person but of one who actively responded. It is necessary to see her as a person of courage—she was human just as we are and must have struggled to make good decisions and right choices. The whole idea of making a decision because of a belief or value is a difficult one for young people to internalize. They can understand, for example, giving their lives for someone they love, but not on principle or faith. This is true, in part, because of the stage adolescents are in as they struggle with their own faith. They start to question and challenge much of what they have been taught; Mary's own response in faith becomes even harder to comprehend. For these reasons, it would be more meaningful to focus on the person of Mary, rather than concentrate on theology or doctrine. This feast occurs during the season of Advent, so it would be appropriate to make connections with it and the coming celebration of Christmas. It is a time of waiting and expectation—much of it focused on the birth of Jesus. And that brings us back to Mary's courageous response and the life she lived without doing any wrong.

This liturgy, though intended for the feast of the Immaculate Conception, may be adapted to other Marian feasts—Our Lady of Guadalupe, for example.

MINISTERS

It is important for the presider of this liturgy to use every opportunity to catechize and make the celebration meaningful for the assembly of young people. There will be a need for a lector, someone to read the intercessions, present gifts, and assist with the entrance procession. It may be necessary to call upon communion ministers from the community of adults if there are not enough students. The celebrant may also want to comment on the insertion of the Glory to God and the Profession of Faith at this Mass.

ENVIRONMENT

The Advent wreath should be displayed at this Mass and deserves some attention from the celebrant as the liturgy begins. Lighting the wreath could be included in the introductory rites of the Mass. Depending on the worship space, it could be enhanced by the use of evergreen branches.

MUSIC

It can be problematic to find that so much Marian music focuses on a medieval, pre–Vatican II image of Mary. The music suggestions in this service try to help us realize that Mary's yes affects our own leaps of faith and how we respond to God's call.

Psalm 103 admits our humanness and God's merciful love for us. Psalm 135 is a beautiful text of praise and recognition of God's beauty. As we process to the table at Communion, we behold one of the greatest works of God: Christ birthed to us through Mary. We hold Christ as a mother holds her child. The final song hearkens us back to the fact that we are in the season of Advent.

LITURGY CHECKLIST

- ❑ Copies of readings, given to readers in advance
- ❑ Copy of intercessions, given to intercessor in advance
- ❑ Appropriate image of Mary
- ❑ Vestments for presider
- ❑ Lectionary, marked and in place
- ❑ Sacramentary, marked and in place
- ❑ Processional cross in place
- ❑ Advent wreath (in Advent)
- ❑ Candles, in place and lit
- ❑ Bread, wine, water, ciboria and communion cups, corporal, purificator(s), finger bowl, finger towel
- ❑ Incense pot, incense resins (in incense boat?), charcoal (lit)
- ❑ Worship aids distributed
- ❑ All involved in the procession are in place—lector, intercessor, any assistants, presider

Other:

ORDER OF WORSHIP

INTRODUCTORY RITES

GATHERING SONG   "I Say Yes, My Lord," songs CD/CS-#10, music book #10.

GREETING

We celebrate the life of Mary, the mother of Jesus,
who from the time of her birth was without sin.
Because we all know how hard it is
to make good choices and right decisions about our behavior,
let us look to Mary as a model for our own lives.

PENITENTIAL RITE   *Sacramentary*, p. 360 (406), invitation A and form A.

GLORY TO GOD   "Glory to God," basics CD/CS1-#3, music book #16.

OPENING PRAYER
Or: *Sacramentary*,
p. 752 (682),
Immaculate Conception

Let us pray.

Almighty God,
you chose Mary to be the Mother of your Son, Jesus.
She lived her whole life without doing any wrong.
As we often struggle to be faithful,
help us to look to her as a model for our own lives.

We ask this through our Lord Jesus Christ, your Son,
who lives and reigns with you and the Holy Spirit,
one God, for ever and ever. R/.

LITURGY OF THE WORD

READING 1   Genesis 3:9–15, 20, *Lectionary #689*
Always observe some silence after the reading.

PSALM   "Psalm 63: As Morning Breaks," basics CD/CS1-#6, music book #19.
Or: "Canticle of the Turning," basics CD/CS2-#13, music book #38.
Observe some silence after the psalm.

READING 2   Ephesians 1:3–6, 11–12, *Lectionary #689*
Always observe some silence after the reading.

GOSPEL ACCLAMATION   "Word of Truth and Life," basics CD/CS2-#6, music book #31.
You may wish to incense the gospel. See the appendix for suggestions.

GOSPEL Luke 1:26–38, *Lectionary #689*

**HOMILY/
REFLECTION NOTES** *As you prepare your homily, you may want to consider the following questions.*

What are some examples from your own life in which you have relied on
   your faith in God to make decisions?
When have you had to trust God's promises to you?
What does it mean to be chosen by God?
What is your greatest obstacle in remaining free from sin?
What image or title of Mary best sums up your experience of her in your
   own life?

PROFESSION OF FAITH

**GENERAL
INTERCESSIONS** Or: "Prayer of the Faithful," basics CD/CS2-#10, music book #35.
*Be sure to add any intentions that are pertinent to your community. The intercessor
should be in place before the presider gives the invitation to pray. These prayers may
be led from the ambo.*

Presider: **Loving God,
we know we need your help in trying to be good.
Hear our needs and prayers.**

Intercessor: **For all women in the Church, let us pray to the Lord: R/.**

**For politicians who debate issues on the rights of women, let us pray
to the Lord: R/.**

**For mothers and grandmothers and aunts and all those who "mother"
young people: that in some way they find strength as they try to do
their best, let us pray to the Lord: R/.**

**For the homeless, especially women and children: that God keep them
safe, let us pray to the Lord: R/.**

**For very young mothers: that they receive the support they need to
provide their children with loving and happy homes, let us pray to the
Lord: R/.**

Other intentions may be added here.

For those who have gone before us, let us pray to the Lord: R/.

The intercessor should face the presider and not leave until the prayer is finished.

Presider: **God our creator and loving parent,
we are confident that you know our needs
and will take care of those we love.
And so we pray in the name of Jesus, your Son. R/.**

LITURGY OF THE EUCHARIST

PREPARATION OF THE ALTAR AND THE GIFTS
"Psalm 103: Deep Down in My Soul, basics CD/CS1-#5, music book #18.

PRAYER OVER THE GIFTS
Or: *Sacramentary,* p. 752 (682), Immaculate Conception

God,
receive our gifts in honor of Mary,
your mother and our model of goodness and faith.
Take them,
and help us to live good lives as your children.

We ask this through Christ our Lord. R/.

EUCHARISTIC PRAYER
Sacramentary, proper preface p. 489 (475), sung preface p. 488 (993); p. 542 (562) Eucharistic Prayer I
"Eucharistic Acclamations," basics CD/CS2-#11, music book #36.

COMMUNION RITE

LORD'S PRAYER

SIGN OF PEACE

BREAKING OF THE BREAD
"Lamb of God," basics CD/CS2-#12, music book #37.
Ask the other ministers to help break bread and pour wine so this rite will not be extended.

COMMUNION SONG
"Psalm 135: We Praise You," basics CD/CS1-#8, music book #21.
Always observe some silence after Communion.

PRAYER AFTER COMMUNION
Sacramentary, p.753 (683), Immaculate Conception

CONCLUDING RITE

GREETING AND BLESSING
"Blessing," basics CD/CS2-#16, music book #41.
Or: *Sacramentary,* p.753 (683), Immaculate Conception

DISMISSAL

RECESSIONAL SONG
"Come, O Come, Emmanuel / O Antiphons," basics CD/CS1-#1, music book #14.

PREPARATION FOR EUCHARISTIC CELEBRATION IN HONOR OF THE BLESSED VIRGIN MARY

GIVE THE GIFT OF FAITH

DATE: **TIME:**

LOCATION:

OVERALL THEME   Mary, model of faith.

SCRIPTURE USED   Genesis 3:9–15, 20 / Ephesians 1:3–6, 11–12 / Luke 1:26–38

SHORT REFLECTION   Much of the preparation for this liturgy should be centered around the person of Mary rather than around theology and doctrine. In looking at the person of Mary, it would be importan certainly to talk about her place in the tradition of the Church and especially emphasize her strong faith in God. If this is a liturgy for the feast of the Immaculate Conception, some discussion about Mary being free from sin might be necessary. Since all of us, young people included, struggle with our human weaknesses, we are very aware of how often we fail to make good choices and appropriate decisions. It is important to remind the students that Mary was indeed a human being and she must have struggled from time to time as well. Because Mary was human, remained free from sin, and even at an early age developed a good deal of faith in God, she would seem to be a person, then, that all people can look to. We all face the daily struggles of choosing good decisions from bad ones. And we certainly can find hope in Mary who placed all her trust in God in spite of very confusing circumstances.

QUESTIONS FOR STUDENTS TO PONDER
1. Why is it hard to be good?
2. What do you do when you have to choose right from wrong? Where does God fit into the decision-making process?
3. When has your faith in God been tested?
4. What helps you when you struggle to believe in God's promises to you?

CLOSING COMMENTS   In spite of the fact that devotion to Mary as the Mother of God has not been a part of the religious education of most young people today, they can still identify with the young woman of the Gospel. They know how hard it is to be good in the face of expectations from parents and school. They know how their faith is tested when confronted by difficult situations. This liturgy reminds them that they have a model to look to: Mary, the mother of Jesus.

Any questions, please contact _____.

PRAYER SERVICE TO BLESS THE NEW YEAR

JANUARY

PREPARATION

The return to school life—and normal life!—after the Christmas holiday is often a difficult one. In some schools, the semester may be winding down and exams are only a couple of weeks away. In other situations, the semester may have ended before Christmas break and the second semester starts with the return. Whatever the circumstances, the nearly two-week absence from the usual routine makes it hard for everyone to refocus their energies on school and other responsibilities, much less the liturgical life of the Church. Gathering for prayer soon after coming back gives everyone the chance to assemble and start the new calendar year as a community of faith by calling upon God to bless not only the year ahead but also the school itself. This would recall a tradition in the Church that blessed homes in honor of the feast of the Epiphany. Most students, and many teachers and youth ministers, too, for that matter, may not be acquainted with this custom. Though the school, or a youth center or catechetical setting, is certainly not a home in the literal sense of the word, figuratively speaking it is "home" for the young people who spend much of their time there.

Depending on the size of the facility or the schedule of the particular institution, there are a couple of ways this service could be handled. One way is to have everyone assemble in whatever place is commonly used, celebrate the service there and have a representative group travel through the building blessing the classrooms and other areas after the service when everyone returns to their own rooms. A second possibility, best with a smaller population and the option followed in the rite presented here, might be to assemble the group in the chapel (or wherever the assembly normally gathers for prayer), complete the service up to the blessing, have the whole group go through the building to bless the classrooms, library, etc., and then return for the conclusion of the service. The procession through the building would include water and incense for blessing.

There may be new students or members to the community. Have a respected student or member of the group welcome the newcomers and introduce them to the rest of the assembly (name, where they are from, etc., depending on size and nature of the group). Conclude the welcoming with a blessing of the newcomers.

A traditional blessing of home and classroom involves the marking of the door or lintel in chalk with "20 + C + M + B + 0__." The numbers represent the year we spend in the this space; the letters recall the traditional names of the three Wise Men—Capser, Balthazar, and Melchior—or the Latin phrase *Christus mansionum benedicat* (May Christ bless this house). This blessing could be included with the blessing with water and incense by the celebrant or performed later by an instructor, class representative, or other regular "occupant" of the room.

MINISTERS

Either option described above would require a presider, an assistant to carry the incense pot, and an assistant to carry the water and aspergill. Since this is a noneucharistic service, a lay minister could serve as presider. It might be appropriate at this time to have the principal or other school leader offer the reflection at the beginning of the New Year. This is especially meaningful if it also marks the start of the new semester. There is a need for a lector and reader for the intercessions as well. The entrance procession should include the processional cross and candles, incense, and a bowl of water and aspergill for the blessing. Since the blessing involves going through the school, the students handling the incense and water might need additional instruction. Peer ministers could do the blessing of the thresholds.

ENVIRONMENT

The worship space will probably still have some of the Christmas look—poinsettias, perhaps a tree or wreath. If there have been no previous decorations, the addition of plants and changing the candles on the Advent wreath to white will help enhance the environment. Be sure that any plants and greens are fresh. Someone may need to be appointed to take care of this prior to the holiday leave.

MUSIC

A new year calls for our yes to God's call to be sung with enthusiasm. It's not unusual for many musicians who have been busy with holiday performances and liturgies to want to "lay out," but they need to renew themselves, too. Perhaps the familiarity of the student musicians with each other and the opportunity to make music and pray together again will allow a spirit of joyful celebration well up within the whole assembly. Celebrate and "push to the other side" of tired and just let loose. Don't hold back—instead, build . . . and even recruit some new members to the ensemble!

LITURGY CHECKLIST

- ❏ Copies of readings, given to readers in advance
- ❏ Copy of intercessions, given to intercessor in advance
- ❏ Vestments for presider
- ❏ Lectionary, marked and in place
- ❏ Sacramentary, marked and in place
- ❏ Book of Blessings, marked and in place
- ❏ Processional cross in place
- ❏ Candles, in place and lit
- ❏ Bowl of water, aspergill
- ❏ Incense pot, incense resins (in incense boat?), charcoal (lit)
- ❏ Worship aids distributed
- ❏ All involved in the procession are in place—lector, intercessor, any assistants, presider

Other:

ORDER OF WORSHIP

INTRODUCTORY RITES

GATHERING SONG   "Yes, Lord," songs CD/CS-#1, music book #1.

GREETING   In the name of the Father, ✠ and of the Son,
and of the Holy Spirit. R/.

If the presider is ordained:
[The Lord be with you. R/.

We gather at the beginning of a new year
to call upon God to bless us
and all of our efforts in the days ahead.
We also ask him to bless this place
and these rooms to which we come every day.

OPENING PRAYER   *If the presider is ordained:*
Or: *Sacramentary,*   [Let us pray.]
p. 906 *(818)*

God of beginnings and endings,
we welcome the opportunity to start a new year filled with
    possibilities and potential.
You have given us the gift of time to make every minute count,
and we ask your blessing upon all the things we do in this building.
Help us to use our time for good:
to build community in the days ahead;
to repair any damaged relationships;
to start our new semester fresh with renewed enthusiasm;
and above all,
to be faithful to our baptism as we continue to learn and grow.

We ask this through our Lord Jesus Christ, your Son,
who lives and reigns with you and the Holy Spirit,
one God, for ever and ever. R/.

LITURGY OF THE WORD

READING 1   Numbers 6:22–27, *Lectionary #841-2*
Always observe some silence after the reading.

PSALM   "Psalm 63: As Morning Breaks," basics CD/CS1-#6, music book #19.
Observe some silence after the psalm.

GOSPEL ACCLAMATION	"Word of Truth and Life," basics CD/CS2-#6, music book #31.
GOSPEL	Luke 19:1–9, *Lectionary* #154 (omit the last sentence/verse in Lectionary)
HOMILY/ REFLECTION NOTES	*As you prepare your reflection, you may want to consider the following questions.*

What are your thoughts at the beginning of a new year?
Do you make resolutions? Why or why not?
When you hear or reflect on the words "the Lord bless you," what meaning do they convey?
To what extent do you identify with Zacchaeus in the gospel reading, who literally goes "out on a limb" to see Jesus?

RENEWAL OF
BAPTISMAL PROMISES
Sacramentary, p. 204–205
(256–257), #46, Renewal
of Baptismal Promises

Dear friends,
as we gather together at the beginning of this new year,
let us renew ourselves
by renewing the promises we made in baptism
when we rejected Satan and his works,
and promised to serve God faithfully
in his holy Catholic Church.

The presider continues with the traditional questions.

The presider then blesses the entire assembly with water—music is playing. When he or she returns, the presider invites everyone to turn to each other making the sign of the cross on the person's forehead closest to him or her.

GENERAL
INTERCESSIONS

Or: "Prayer of the Faithful," basics CD/CS2-#10, music book #35.

Presider:

We thank God for this new year
and another chance to live and grow in his presence.
We bring our prayers and needs for the days to come.

Intercessor:

Jesus, your Son, made the earth his home. That all the places we call home are filled with the presence and light of Christ, let us pray to the Lord: R/.

God, you created the days and nights that grow into the weeks of new years. Bless each day of the year ahead with hope and life. Let us pray to the Lord: R/.

Lord God, you bless us and give us your peace. For all those whose lives are lacking in peace, let us pray to the Lord: R/.

You promised us a home with you when our lives have ended. For those we love who have died: that they enjoy eternal peace with you, let us pray to the Lord: R/.

95

LORD'S PRAYER   As members of the same family we pray: R/.

If there is to be no introduction and blessing of newcomers to the community, continue below with concluding rite.

The presider may invite forward the one who will introduce the newcomers. After the introduction of the newcomers, the presider invites them to stand for a blessing:

May the road rise to meet you.
May the wind be always at your back.
May the sun shine warm upon your face,
the rains fall soft upon your fields,
and may God hold you always in the palm of his hand.

CONCLUDING RITE

GREETING AND BLESSING
Sacramentary, p. 570 (529),
#3 Solemn Blessing

Let us once again call upon God to bless us.

If choosing the second option, after the blessing over the people and the year, the entire group goes through the school (prayers and directions located below with the recessional song) and returns for the rest of the service. During the procession: "Now," songs CD/CS-#13, music book #13.

Presider: Let us praise God,
who fills our hearts, homes, and school (church) with peace.
    Blessed be God forever.

All: Blessed be God forever.

Presider: Jesus, the Son of God, made his home among us.
We ask God to bless us and the year to come
so we may spread the light of Jesus to all we meet.

If the presider is ordained:
[Let us pray.]

Lord God,
creator of all times and seasons,
all nations came to know your Son because they followed the star.
Bless us who gather here each day in your name
to continue with courage and hope
as we follow the light of Christ.
Bless all of our efforts and work here in this school (place).
Bless, too, each day of the year ahead
with your grace and presence.

We ask this through Christ our Lord. R/.

DISMISSAL   *If the presider is not ordained (crossing oneself):*
May the Lord bless us,
protect us from all evil
and bring us to everlasting life. R/.

RECESSIONAL SONG   "We Are Called," songs CD/CS-#6, music book #6.

Once the second verse starts, the presider, with assistants carrying the incense pot and water, leaves the space and goes to each classroom with a small representative group. The assistant holding the incense pot adds incense as needed.

Upon arriving at each door, the presider says:

Bless this room and all that use it.
Fill them with the light of Christ
and may their concern for others reflect your love. R/.

If room being blessed is occupied, have four singers along who can lead the refrain of "We Are Called" at the conclusion of the blessing.

The presider sprinkles the doorway with water and proceeds in the same manner with other rooms to be blessed; the designated person marks the door or lintel if this is to be done at this time.

PREPARATION FOR PRAYER SERVICE TO BLESS THE NEW YEAR

GIVE THE GIFT OF A NEW YEAR

DATE: **TIME:**

LOCATION:

OVERALL THEME   Calling on God's presence and a blessing on the new year.

SCRIPTURE USED   Numbers 6:22–27 / Luke 19:1–9

SHORT REFLECTION   The tradition of ritual blessings may not be familiar to many young people. The beginning of the new year offers an opportunity to acquaint them with this rich practice at an appropriate time. They are returning from Christmas break and the reentry from a vacation mode is often difficult. Gathering the community for prayer at this time gives a focal point and allows them to acknowledge the new year in the context of faith. Young people certainly can identify the significance of the passage of time, since high school is a period of so many transitions and milestones. They may welcome the chance to call upon God to bless the year ahead and whatever it may hold for them. It might even be that some of vacation time with family was difficult. Perhaps the expectations of a happy holiday were not entirely realized. If it's a new semester, the opportunity to start a new class with a new teacher and a clean slate is most welcome. The reading from Numbers should be especially applicable in this regard: "The Lord look upon you kindly and give you peace." Finally, the blessing of homes, which is another tradition that may be unfamiliar, is extended here to include the classrooms of the school. We call on God in this new year to bless even the rooms we use.

QUESTIONS FOR STUDENTS TO PONDER
1. Did you make any resolutions for the new year? What are they? Are they realistic?
2. What do you look forward to in the coming year?
3. What "mistakes" would you like to correct or do differently in this new year?
4. What blessings from God are you in need of as you face a new year?
5. What blessings do you pray for in regard to those you love?

CLOSING COMMENTS   Like the Magi who traveled far to find the promised King, we search for God in our lives. Sometimes we forget that he is indeed here among us. He lives in each one of us. His blessings go with us into the new year. We are aware of his presence even as we go in and out of our classrooms each day.

Any questions, please contact _____.

EUCHARISTIC CELEBRATION OF MARTIN LUTHER KING DAY

(OR IN CELEBRATION OF BLACK HISTORY MONTH)

JANUARY / FEBRUARY

PREPARATION

GETTING STARTED

Because Martin Luther King Day is a national holiday and is probably observed with a day off from school, the message he embraced and the dream of equality to which he was so dedicated is one that should be celebrated by a community prayer experience. Whether the celebration is on or near the actual day of observance or is part of a schoolwide celebration of diversity or multiculturalism, this message needs to be connected to the mandate of Jesus to love one another. We look to Jesus as an example of someone who did not discriminate when he helped people. He reached out to everyone regardless of whether or not they were considered among the socially acceptable. This message is so important for young people to hear—that all people are worthy of love and respect, no matter who they are. Jesus, Martin Luther King, Jr., and Mahatma Gandhi are examples of those who gave their lives to achieve peace without raising a weapon, and showed that all people are equal in the eyes of God. The readings selected for this liturgy focus on that aspect of their work—that they were peacemakers. Though we celebrate and break bread together as a community, we know that working at building a real community is difficult. We all need the help and support of each other to accept the challenge of embracing diversity and celebrating it rather than letting it divide us as a people.

At this liturgy the gathered young people and adults are asked to make a pledge to be peacemakers by opposing racism in all its forms. In the introduction to the pledge, individual schools may want to include other inspirations—the founder or patron saint of the sponsoring congregation, the namesake of the school, a line from the mission statement—something that connects this pledge to the faith heritage of this particular community. The introduction to the pledge is another chance to highlight the diversity in the community in a more dramatic way. It is also a time when we recognize the struggles of the African American community and other minority groups in our society.

Depending on the makeup of your community, you may choose not to have a eucharistic service and instead hold a Liturgy of the Word celebrating Black History Month. This is a time for racial lines to fall and for all to come together as one population with all the other cultures.

MINISTERS

It is important that members of the community who represent the racial and ethnic diversity of the school carry out the visible ministries in this liturgy. This could also be an opportunity to invite a priest of, or who ministers to, a different ethnic background from the majority population of the school or parish community. Select readers who accurately represent the makeup of your community. Position them in different places in the assembly from which to read the individual lines, so that they come from the assembly rather than being seen as apart from it. If the space is large, their voices will need amplification. How this is accomplished will depend on the resources available in the community.

ENVIRONMENT

The use of flags and colors representing the racial and ethnic makeup of the school community would be an appropriate enhancement of the worship space.

MUSIC

Music selections for this service were chosen in an attempt to be sensitive to the African American heritage. A local African American parish musician may be able to come in and show the music group how to make music having the faith-filled spirit we have come to love. A local college or university may also be able to put you in touch with experienced musicians who could take on this daunting task.

LITURGY CHECKLIST

- ❑ Copies of readings, given to readers in advance
- ❑ Copy of intercessions, given to intercessor in advance
- ❑ Vestments for presider
- ❑ Lectionary, marked and in place
- ❑ Sacramentary, marked and in place
- ❑ Additional microphones, if needed
- ❑ Processional cross in place
- ❑ Candles, in place and lit
- ❑ Flags or banners and stands in place
- ❑ Bread, wine, water, ciboria and communion cups, coporal, purificator(s), finger bowl, finger towel
- ❑ Worship aids distributed (including pledge statements)
- ❑ All involved in the procession are in place—lector, intercessor, flag or banner bearers, any assistants, presider

Other:

ORDER OF WORSHIP

INTRODUCTORY RITES

GATHERING SONG

"He Came Down / We Are Marching (Siyahumba)," basics CD/CS1-#2, music book #15. *During Lent omit "He Came Down" portion.*

GREETING

PENITENTIAL RITE
Or: *Sacramentary,*
p. 360 *(406)*, invitation
B and form C-ii *(c-2)*

My friends,
we gather in the name of Jesus,
who was the greatest peacemaker of all time
and never excluded anyone from his table.

Jesus, you taught us that God is the Father of all people.
Lord, have mercy. R/.

Jesus, you showed us by your life that we should not let
   our differences divide us.
Christ, have mercy. R/.

Jesus, you ask God to forgive us when we are not peacemakers.
Lord, have mercy. R/.

May almighty God have mercy on us,
forgive us our sins,
and bring us to everlasting life. R/.

GLORIA

"Glory to God," basics CD/CS1-#3, music book #16.
Omit during Lent.

OPENING PRAYER
Or: *Sacramentary,*
p. 902 *(815)*, #22,
For Peace and Justice

Let us pray.

God of justice,
we are thankful for people like Martin Luther King, Jr.,
who gave up their lives to work so tirelessly for peace
   and the equality of all people.
Help us to follow his example
and that of your Son, Jesus,
who lives and reigns with you and the Holy Spirit,
one God, for ever and ever. R/.

LITURGY OF THE WORD

READING 1

Colossians 3:12–15, *Lectionary #832-2*
Always observe some silence after the reading.

101

PSALM   "Psalm 34: Taste and See," basics CD/CS1-#7, music book #20.
Observe some silence after the psalm.

GOSPEL ACCLAMATION   "Word of Truth and Life," basics CD/CS2-#6, music book #31.
During Lent: "Open Our Ears," basics CD/CS2-#5, music book #30.

GOSPEL   Matthew 5:1–12, *Lectionary* #835-1

HOMILY/ REFLECTION NOTES   *As you prepare your homily, you may want to consider these questions.*
What is your understanding of the work of a peacemaker?
What do you think is the hardest about making peace—personally or on more global levels?
Why are people like King and Gandhi the targets of assassins when they themselves espouse nonviolence?
How can you or any individual be one of the "blessed" or "happy" who are the peacemakers?
Have you ever directly experienced peaceful nonviolence on a personal level?

RITUAL   Commitment/pledge to continue the work of Martin Luther King, Jr., in our community.

The presider introduces the pledge in these or similar words.

Presider: **We make all kinds of commitments in life
to people, to jobs, to following through on a goal or plan.
Today, as a community who professes faith in Jesus and tries
   to live as he did,
we make a commitment to be the kind of peacemakers he asks
   us to be.**

After each of the following proclamations, the assembly sings the refrain of "I Say Yes, My Lord," *songs CD/CS-#10, music book #10.*

Three or more readers are positioned in different places in the assembly. Individually, they stand and proclaim.

Reader 1:   **In the spirit of Jesus, who reached out to all and loved so much that he gave up his life, we sing . . .**

Reader 2:   **In the spirit of all those people throughout history who sacrificed themselves in the name of justice, we sing . . .**

Reader 3:   **In the spirit of Martin Luther King, Jr., whose dream inspired so many to work for justice and equality, we sing . . .**

Insert inspirations specific to the community here, with sung response.

Presider: **Please stand.**

Starting today,
will you do the best you can to educate others and yourselves
about the importance of respecting and celebrating diversity?

All: **We will.**

Presider: **Do you promise to take a stand against discrimination in all its forms
and speak out against racism and intolerance?**

All: **We do.**

Presider: **Will you examine your own attitudes and behaviors
so that you can be an example to others of acceptance and tolerance,
and following the example of Jesus,
will you be people of peace
and put your love of God into action?**

All: **We will.**

Presider: **We ask Jesus, our brother,
to help us in this difficult work.
Let us sing together . . .**

Assembly sings full rendition of "I Say Yes, My Lord," *songs CD/CS-#10,
music book #10.*

LITURGY OF THE EUCHARIST

**PREPARATION OF THE
ALTAR AND THE GIFTS**

"All Things New," basics CD/CS2-#15, music book #40, *or by the ensemble only,
especially if whole assembly has just sung above responses.*

**PRAYER OVER
THE GIFTS**
Or: *Sacramentary,*
p. 902 (815), #22,
For Peace and Justice

**God of peace,
we bring you our gifts of bread and wine.
We also bring ourselves
and ask that you help us to be people of peace
who accept all people in the name of Jesus,
who lives and reigns with you for ever and ever. R/.**

EUCHARISTIC PRAYER

Eucharistic Prayer for Masses for Various Needs and Occasions IV: Jesus, the
Compassion of God; or *Sacramentary,* p. 556 (517), Eucharistic Prayer IV
"Eucharistic Acclamations," basics CD/CS2-#11, music book #36.

COMMUNION RITE

LORD'S PRAYER

SIGN OF PEACE

BREAKING OF THE BREAD
"Lamb of God," basics CD/CS2-#12, music book #37.
Ask the other ministers to help break bread and pour wine so this rite will not be extended.

COMMUNION SONG
"We Are Called," songs CD/CS-#6, music book #6.
Always observe some silence after Communion.

PRAYER AFTER COMMUNION
Or: *Sacramentary,* p. 902 (815), #22, For Peace and Justice

Let us pray.

Loving God,
joined as a community of believers who share Communion
at the same table,
help us to extend this community and acceptance to all people.

We ask this through Christ our Lord. R/.

CONCLUDING RITE

GREETING AND BLESSING
Or: *Sacramentary,* p. 574 (532), #11, Ordinary Time II

"Blessing," basics CD/CS2-#16, music book #41.

DISMISSAL

RECESSIONAL SONG
"Send Down the Fire," basics CD/CS2-#2, music book #27.

PREPARATION FOR EUCHARISTIC CELEBRATION OF MARTIN LUTHER KING DAY

GIVE THE GIFT OF JUSTICE

DATE: **TIME:**

LOCATION:

OVERALL THEME   Being peacemakers who embrace diversity.

SCRIPTURE USED   Colossians 3:12–15 / Matthew 5:1–12

SHORT REFLECTION   The observance of Martin Luther King Day may be seen as simply a day off in the school calendar, like Presidents' Day; however, the power and strength of Dr. King's message provides a teachable moment in which we can connect his life-work with the gospel message of Jesus found in the Beatitudes. Jesus tells us that happy are the peacemakers, the poor in spirit, the lowly, the sorrowing. This is a message that runs counter to the ones with which young people are bombarded in the media and all aspects of society. There are many forces at work here: adolescents struggling to find themselves in the sameness of the group are not often open to those who are different; issues that surface on an interpersonal level, which often lead to fights; the strong mandate to look out for ourselves, which leaves little room to be welcoming persons of peace. It then becomes more important to help make the connections between the Gospel and the call to be people who are accepting of others, who do turn the other cheek, who do not raise a hand in violence but find alternative ways of settling differences. We want to remind adolescents that this peace-making work is not a creation of some individuals but an integral part of our faith heritage.

QUESTIONS FOR STUDENTS TO PONDER
1. Why is it hard to be a peacemaker?
2. What changes do you have to make in your life to be a person of peace?
3. What can you do in your own life to be more accepting of others?
4. What steps can you take to be a person who lives out the message of the Gospel?
5. Who in your life is an example of a peacemaker?

CLOSING COMMENTS   It is difficult be the kind of person described in the Beatitudes. Whenever we go counter to the prevailing societal messages, we run the risk of being misunderstood. All of us, especially young people, need to be reminded that they are not in this alone and should look to Jesus and their faith community for support.

Any questions, please contact _____.

ASH WEDNESDAY PRAYER SERVICE
FEBRUARY / MARCH

PREPARATION

GETTING STARTED

The beginning of Lent provides catechists, religion instructors, campus ministers, and youth ministers a built-in opportunity to bring together a comprehensive program in spiritual development that includes both prayer and catechesis. Lent in itself has a rich history of being a time of renewal, of interior "spring cleaning," of penance and fasting, of giving something up. Whatever focus is chosen, whatever program is developed, Ash Wednesday is the starting point. The readings center on a change of heart and introduce the behaviors with which to achieve this change: fasting, almsgiving, and prayer. Throughout the history of the Church, all of these terms and ideas have taken on a variety of interpretations. As we approach this liturgical season, it is necessary to explore the implications for young people today. The use of ashes as a symbol should be explored in class prior to the service and receive at least some attention during the service itself. Students may need to be reminded of the historical significance of ashes as a sign of penance, but also they need to know that ashes are for us a sign of our willingness to enter into the spirit of Lent. We acknowledge that indeed we are a flawed people who need to make some changes in order to more fully celebrate our redemption and salvation at Easter.

The service includes the complete Liturgy of the Word, followed by the distribution of ashes. In order to facilitate the distribution of ashes, it might be necessary to invite teachers or student eucharistic ministers to assist with this. The first reading could be proclaimed using two or more readers. One reader begins with the first set of verses (12–14). Then, alternate readers on each of the command statements. Both readers can read the last verse together.

MINISTERS

Two or three readers will be needed to proclaim Scripture and read the intercessions. If two readers are used for the reading from Joel, a third will be needed for intercessions. In addition to the processional cross and candles, the bowls of ashes should be part of the entrance procession. Depending on the number of people in attendance and the size of the worship space, those ministers (teacher, students, staff) designated to distribute ashes should each carry a bowl or container of them. The presider and lectors follow. It is important that those distributing ashes memorize the statement to be said.

Consider having the assembly sign each other with ashes during the rite. The first group of assigned ministers comes forward for the blessing of the ashes; they then go to their assigned station. As members of the assembly come forward to be signed, the original minister signs the first person in line. The assigned minister remains holding the bowl of ashes and repeats the words, but each member of the assembly remains after being signed to sign the person behind before returning to his or her seat.

If the presider is not a priest, he or she needs to be someone who is comfortable leading prayer in the community as well as sharing a reflection on Scripture.

ENVIRONMENT

The color of Lent is purple and should be used to enhance the worship space. Ashes should be placed in clay or glass bowls, enough for each person who will assist with the distribution. In keeping with the season, everything else should be simple—rocks, branches. The bowl of water and aspergill need to be accessible to the presider for the blessing of the ashes.

MUSIC

The text for "Now" comes from the reading of the day; use it also as a penitential litany. Since *alleluia* is not sung during Lent as part of our "liturgical fast," "Open Our Ears" serves as our preparation to hear the gospel reading. A procession through the worship space with the Lectionary and incense honors the word of God—and the extended acclamation of "Open Our Ears" breaks the rhythm of a sung Alleluia. The distribution of ashes may call for a music selection that can build and lend itself to improvisation. The Taizé chant "O Lord, Hear Our Prayer" lends itself well to the moment, and it can be woven into the general intercessions. "You Are Mine" is a fine piece of music to send us forth to do the acts of the Lenten mission.

LITURGY CHECKLIST

- ❑ Copies of readings, given to readers in advance
- ❑ Copy of intercessions, given to intercessor in advance
- ❑ Vestments for presider
- ❑ Lectionary, marked and in place
- ❑ Sacramentary, marked and in place
- ❑ Processional cross in place
- ❑ Candles, in place and lit
- ❑ Bowls of ashes
- ❑ Bowl of water and aspergill
- ❑ Container of water and towels to be used by those distributing ashes
- ❑ Worship aids distributed
- ❑ All involved in the procession are in place—lector, intercessor, ministers of ashes, any assistants, presider

Other:

ORDER OF WORSHIP

INTRODUCTORY RITES

GATHERING SONG "Now," songs CD/CS-#13, music book #13.

GREETING
Or: *Book of Blessings*,
p. 704, #1663

As we begin this season of Lent today,
we know that we need to make changes in our lives
in order to be the best persons we can be.
We often let our families, our friends, and ourselves down by
the choices we make.
And so we ask God to be present with us
as we make a sincere effort to change our hearts.

Pause briefly in silence.

OPENING PRAYER
Sacramentary, p. 76 (148),
first choice

Forgiving God,
you know only too well how often we have failed
to live up to our call to be followers of Jesus, your Son.
We welcome this season of Lent as a time to make some changes,
to renew our commitment to follow the Gospel,
and so prepare ourselves for the celebration of Easter.
Help us with your presence and grace to make the changes needed
in our lives.

We ask this through our Lord Jesus Christ, your Son,
who lives and reigns with you and the Holy Spirit,
one God, for ever and ever. R/.

LITURGY OF THE WORD

READING 1 Joel 2:12–18, *Lectionary #220*
Always observe some silence after the reading.

PSALM "Psalm 80: Lord, Let Us See Your Kindness," basics CD/CS1-#4,
music book #17.
Observe some silence after the psalm.

READING 2 2 Corinthians 5:20–6:2, *Lectionary #220*
Always observe some silence after the reading.

GOSPEL ACCLAMATION "Open Our Ears," basics CD/CS2-#5, music book #30.

GOSPEL Matthew 6:1–6, 16–18, *Lectionary #220*

HOMILY/ REFLECTION NOTES

You may want to consider the following questions as you prepare your reflection.
In your own experience, how have you observed Lent? In the past? Now?
What changes in your own understanding of Lent contribute to the
    way you observe it?
What are some ways you are challenged to change your heart?
What is the significance of ashes for you personally?

BLESSING AND DISTRIBUTION OF ASHES
Or: *Sacramentary,* pp. 76–77 (148–149)

My sisters and brothers,
we lift our hearts in prayer
that God will bless these ashes.
We wear this mark of ashes
as a sign of our willingness to change our hearts this Lenten season.

Pause for silent prayer.

Loving God,
bless these ashes,
which remind us of the need each of us has to change our hearts
    and return to you.
We ask that you bless all of us gathered here
so that we may be able to keep the resolutions we make during
    this Lenten season.

We ask this through Christ our Lord. R/.

The presider sprinkles the ashes with holy water.

Appropriate songs, such as "O Lord, Hear Our Prayer," basics CD/CS2-#8, music book #33, may be sung during the distribution of ashes. If using "O Lord, Hear Our Prayer," continue through the general intercessions.

As the ministers place ashes on the forehead of each person, they say:
Turn away from sin and be faithful to the gospel.

When finished with the distribution of ashes, the ministers hands are washed.

GENERAL INTERCESSIONS
Presider:

Continue singing "O Lord, Hear Our Prayer."
Or: *Sacramentary,* p. 998 (903), #5, Lent I
My friends,
let us continue to lift our hearts to God
as we pray for our own needs
and for those of all God's people.

Intercessor:
For all followers of Jesus: that they use this season of Lent to return with their whole hearts to God, let us pray to the Lord: R/. *(refrain)*

For those who struggle to believe and those who have lost hope: that this Lent remind them of Jesus' victory over death, let us pray to the Lord: R/. *(refrain)*

109

For all of us gathered here: that we support each other's effort to keep the resolutions we make today, let us pray to the Lord: R/. *(refrain)*

That we follow the example of Jesus and open our hearts in forgiveness to those who have hurt us, let us pray to the Lord: R/. *(refrain)*

Other intentions may be added here:

That those who have died may find peace in God's presence, let us pray to the Lord: R/. *(refrain)*

LORD'S PRAYER   Gathered together to begin this holy season of Lent, we join to pray in the way Jesus taught us: R/.

SIGN OF PEACE

CONCLUDING RITE

GREETING AND BLESSING
Or: "Blessing," basics CD/CS2-#16, music book #41. *Sacramentary*, p. 580 (538), #6

If the presider is not ordained (crossing oneself):
May the Lord bless us, protect us from all evil and bring us to everlasting life.

DISMISSAL   Go in the peace of Christ. R/.

CLOSING SONG   "You Are Mine," songs CD/CS-#9, music book #9.

PREPARATION FOR ASH WEDNESDAY PRAYER SERVICE AND DISTRIBUTION OF ASHES

GIVE THE GIFT OF METANOIA

DATE: **TIME:**

LOCATION:

OVERALL THEME   Change of heart.

SCRIPTURE USED   Joel 2:12–18 / 2 Corinthians 5:20–6:2 / Matthew 6:1–6, 16–18

SHORT REFLECTION   The season of Lent may conjure up all kinds of memories for adults about giving up favorite or not-so-favorite food items as a young child. It would be good to explore the reason that this has been part of the Lenten tradition so that the teens understand that in foregoing these special treats they are relinquishing some of the control that this item has on them. Thus, they are opening themselves to the presence of God simply because there is more "room" for God to enter. It would also be good to talk about the traditions of Lent relative to this "giving up." We go without so that we might know what someone else who is hungry all the time might feel. We take the money we would have spent on soft drinks, candy, pizza, etc., and donate it to some cause. All of this is a form of fasting from something and almsgiving—we refrain from some food, we give to those who are less fortunate. Lent is also a time to concentrate on our personal interior lives—the change of heart that is talked about in the first and second readings. We try to make time for more prayer, or more meaningful prayer, so that this dimension of our lives is changed. We are also called to look at those rough edges that may need to change: Is it our tone of voice? Our propensity for untruth? Our use of bad language? The ashes that are placed on our foreheads remind us of the need to change our heart in some way during this time before Easter.

QUESTIONS FOR STUDENTS TO PONDER
1. What are the things in your life that sometimes have control over you?
2. What changes can you make to return more fully to God this Lenten season?
3. When you think about your friends and those closest to you, what might they tell you that you should work on?
4. Where would you start in your personal "spring cleaning"?
5. What areas of your life could benefit from a renewed relationship with God?

CLOSING COMMENTS   At its start, Lent seems like a very long season to go without something or to work on getting rid of bad habits. But even if we fail at our resolutions from time to time, Lent gives us a chance to take stock of our interior selves, our faith lives, and to see the work that needs to be done in order to really be prepared for the Resurrection.

Any questions, please contact _____.

LENTEN RECONCILIATION SERVICE
MARCH / APRIL

PREPARATION

GETTING STARTED

As in Advent, the rhythm of the church year provides yet another opportunity for reconciliation. Given the size of any Catholic high school or high school parish program and the availability of priests, to offer the sacrament itself may not be realistic. In lieu of that, offering a prayer experience that focuses on the theme of forgiveness might be the impetus for young people to seek out the sacrament in their parish churches. Some adaptations could be made in this service to accommodate sacramental reconciliation, if needed. Since relationships are so integral to the lives of teens, the gospel of the Prodigal Son should resonate with their experience. As teens are in the process of growing and changing, seeking their own identities as adult persons, they will often rub up against standards set by parents and teachers. They are also finding their way in their spiritual lives, which often leads to doubts about God and faith. Given these realities, as well as the many relationships in their lives that are also changing in focus, taking out some quiet time to reflect and ask for forgiveness is appropriate any time during Lent. Having already set the stage for conversion and change of heart on Ash Wednesday, this service extends those themes and asks us to look at our lives and realize where it is that we need a new heart and new spirit, like the prophet Ezekiel calls us to in the first reading. Above all, though we recognize our sinfulness and our need for reconciliation, we also praise and thank God for the unconditional forgiveness that is ours. We are awed by the gospel story that gives us the image of the elderly man running out to embrace his wayward son. We all need to be reminded that this is the kind of forgiveness and acceptance that is our heritage as well.

For further information on the sacramental confession and absolution and penitential services, as well as alternate themes and texts, see The Rite of Penance, especially noting Appendixes II and III.

MINISTERS

Though the ideal presider would be a priest who could offer the sacrament, if that is not possible, a lay minister could preside over a prayer service. In addition to the role of leader, a lector is needed for the Ezekiel reading. A student reader or the presider could lead the invocations after praying the Confiteor (I confess) together. Ideally, the presider is also able to share some reflections; if that is not the case, another adult in the community could be invited to do so. If the service is intended for a large group in a bigger space, an entrance procession with cross, candles, ashes, and water bowl is suggested.

Consider asking one of the young people to share his or her own experiences of seeking forgiveness and the emotions he or she experienced before, during, and after the reconciliation. Many "adult" stories seem foreign to younger people, while a peer's story of family life, dating, school pressure, or social demands can have a more meaningful effect. The homilist can work with the young "storyteller" so that the narration has a beginning, middle, and end, and a connection to the Scripture reading and focus of the service.

ENVIRONMENT

Since this is Lent, purple is used to enhance the worship space. A bowl of water, which is also needed for the ritual section, and a bowl of ashes would further emphasize the ideas of a clean heart and change of heart that were introduced on Ash Wednesday.

MUSIC

Keep the music simple and more of a means to identify the shadow side of ourselves that needs forgiveness.

Again, the issue of bilingual music comes into play. Dare yourselves to try bilingual singing if you are not in the habit. Many of the singers on the recording for this project do not speak Spanish, but they understood the meaning of the song and were thus able to interpret the spirit through the syllables of another language.

Note that in "Come and Fill Our Hearts" there are two measures of alleluia. To avoid these during Lent, simply repeat the text from the end of the first phrase during these measures ("you alone are ho-ly").

Musically, the examination of conscience modulates from D major to e minor of the general intercessions. An experienced solo keyboardist or guitarist can make this transition smoothly during the intervening prayer of forgiveness.

The closing song needs to reflect the energy of our being sent forth into the world renewed to make a difference in that world. Although human, we will continue to try to follow the way of Christ!

LITURGY CHECKLIST

- ❑ Copies of readings, given to readers in advance
- ❑ Copy of intercessions, given to intercessor in advance
- ❑ Vestments for presider
- ❑ Lectionary, marked and in place
- ❑ Sacramentary, marked and in place
- ❑ Bowl of water
- ❑ Bowl of ashes
- ❑ Processional cross in place
- ❑ Candles, in place and lit

Other:

ORDER OF WORSHIP

INTRODUCTORY RITES

[handwritten: There will be an opening song]

[handwritten: not this one]
"If," songs CD/CS-#11, music book #11.

✓ We gather in this season of Lent,
a time of renewal, conversion, and change of heart.
We know only too well our own need for forgiveness from God
    and from those we love,
so when Easter comes
we will be ready with renewed hearts and spirits.

If presider is ordained:
[Let us pray.]

Or: *Sacramentary,*
p. 924 (835), first choice

✓ Merciful God,
we come to you much as the prodigal son in today's gospel reading—
looking for forgiveness.
Like the young man in the story,
we are overwhelmed by your love and acceptance
even when we have failed.
During this season of Lent,
we want to return to you.
Give us a clean heart as we begin again.

We ask this through our Lord Jesus Christ, your Son,
who lives and reigns with you and the Holy Spirit,
one God, for ever and ever. R/.

LITURGY OF THE WORD

✓ Ezekiel 36:23–28, *Lectionary* #422
Always observe some silence after the reading.

[handwritten: will be sung]
"Psalm 80: Lord, Let Us See Your Kindness," basics CD/CS1-#4,
music book #17.
Observe some silence after the psalm.

"Open Our Ears," basics CD/CS2-#5, music book #30.

✓ Luke 15:1–3, 11–32, *Lectionary* #890-4

**HOMILY/
REFLECTION NOTES**

You may want to use the following questions to help in preparing your reflection.
When have you had an experience like the prodigal son and the
   unconditional forgiveness he received?
What did that experience feel like? How did you respond?
Why is forgiveness so difficult to offer but easy to receive?
What does it mean to have a clean heart?
What obstacles do you face in seeking and offering forgiveness?

**EXAMINATION OF
CONSCIENCE**

**Take a few moments of quiet reflection.
Look into your own heart and your own life
and identify the areas in need of forgiveness.**

Soft music will be playing while reflecting questions will be read for students to reflect on

*Play some music here, e.g., an instrumental reprise of "Come and Fill Our Hearts,"
basics CD/CS2-#9, music book #34.*

*Or: Adapt a spoken examination of conscience, especially if the sacrament will be cel-
ebrated, from Appendix III: Form of Examination of Conscience from Rite of
Penance.*

**As you complete your reflection,
please come forward and sign yourself with the water from the bowl.**

*After all have had a chance to come forward and bless themselves, continue with the
prayer of forgiveness.*

**PRAYER OF
FORGIVENESS**

**In this season of renewal
we pray to our loving and forgiving God,
so that we might celebrate the Resurrection with a new heart
   and a new spirit.
Let us kneel and pray.**

All: **I confess to Almighty God and to you, my brothers and sisters. . .**

**GENERAL
INTERCESSIONS**

Or: "Prayer of the Faithful," basics CD/CS2-#10, music book #35
*Though not intercessions in the usual sense, these invocations acknowledge our
need for God in order to make a positive change in our lives.*

Presider: **Let us call upon God's presence to help us in renewing our lives
and changing our hearts.**

Intercessor: **The response to each invocation is: Create a clean heart in me. R/.**

When we withhold love. R/.

**When we turn away from good choices and make ones harmful
to others or ourselves. R/.**

When we allow others to lead us into troublesome situations. R/.

When we don't exercise good judgment. R/.

All sing "O Lord, Hear Our Prayer," basics CD/CS2-#8, music book #33.

When we get lazy. R/.

When we cause pain instead of joy in the lives of those closest
to us. R/.

When we lose faith. R/.

When we let ourselves be overwhelmed by discouragement. R/.

All sing "O Lord, Hear Our Prayer," basics CD/CS2-#8, music book #33.

LORD'S PRAYER

Presider: Let us now,
as brothers and sisters of Jesus,
join our hands and hearts
and pray to our loving and forgiving Father.

All: Our Father. . .

*If the sacrament of penance is to be celebrated, individual confession and absolution
take place now.*

SIGN OF PEACE

CONCLUDING RITE

GREETING AND
BLESSING AND PRAYER

Forgiving God,
we praise you for standing with us today
and giving us the gifts of peace and reconciliation.
We thank you for taking us back
and forgiving us just as the father embraced his prodigal son.
We celebrate this opportunity to start over
and will try to live as your children.

We ask this through Christ our Lord. R/.

BLESSING
Or: "Blessing," basics
CD/CS2-#16,
music book #41.
Sacramentary, p. 574 (533),
Solemn Blessing #12,
Ordinary Time III

If the presider is not ordained (crossing oneself):
May the Lord bless us,
protect us from all evil
and bring us to everlasting life.

DISMISSAL Go in the peace of Christ. R/.

CLOSING SONG "Come and Follow Me," songs CD/CS-#3, music book #3.

PREPARATION FOR LENTEN RECONCILIATION SERVICE

GIVE THE GIFT OF RECONCILIATION

DATE: **TIME:**

LOCATION:

OVERALL THEME   Celebrating God's forgiveness.

SCRIPTURE USED   Ezekiel 36:23–28 / Luke 15:1–3, 11–32

SHORT REFLECTION   The themes of forgiveness and reconciliation are not strangers to adolescent life. As part of the emotional, physical, and spiritual upheaval that is taking place in their lives, it seems young people are often offending someone, repairing or ending a relationship, or smoothing over someone's ruffled feathers. Along the way, they are getting lessons on the importance of forgiveness. But there may exist an empty space in spite of all this. Friends will only take them back so many times; the best of relationships seem to come to a premature end. Relationships with parents may be unstable for long periods of time. Providing time in the middle of Lent for some reflection on God's unconditional love and forgiveness can deliver a much-needed oasis for some teens. They may see themselves as having failed a number of people and get discouraged. A prayer experience allows them to face their own failings honestly but also to hear that no matter what, God's love and forgiveness doesn't have any limits. As they reflect on areas in their own lives that need to change, they are also invited to celebrate this unconditional forgiveness.

QUESTIONS FOR STUDENTS TO PONDER
1. Have you ever been forgiven like the son in the gospel reading?
2. What holds you back from asking for forgiveness from those you have hurt?
3. Is it easy to forgive someone who has hurt your? Why? Why not?
4. What do you need to change in your own life so as to be more open to God's love?
5. How are the resolutions you made on Ash Wednesday working out? Are they leading you to a change of heart?

CLOSING COMMENTS   Whether or not teenagers avail themselves of the sacrament of reconciliation, they still need a formal experience in which they have a chance to acknowledge their failures and sins, and seek forgiveness. By allowing them quiet time in which to reflect on and apply the words of Scripture to their own lives, we provide them with an opportunity to renew their relationship with God.

Any questions, please contact _____.

EUCHARISTIC CELEBRATION
OF THE ASCENSION

MAY

PREPARATION

GETTING STARTED

This solemnity may occur just as school is ending or very close to the end of the academic year. Depending on when it falls in the liturgical calendar, it may actually serve as the end of the school year liturgy as well. The celebration itself focuses on Jesus' return to God, which resonates with the closure and departure students experience as they leave for the summer; however, the focus here will remain specifically on the liturgical celebration, since there is a baccalaureate liturgy and an end-of-the-year/leave-taking service included in this collection. This liturgy would also work well for a parish youth liturgy for Ascension.

The feast of the Ascension reminds us that Jesus was physically present to his friends and disciples for forty days after his resurrection. Before leaving and returning to God, he promised his followers that he would not leave them alone. The promise of Jesus was that the Spirit would come; his presence would be with us always. The call given to all of us is that we are to be Jesus' witnesses now that he is not present to us. The kind of witness we are to be is not just the kind who sees and reports an event, but the kind that, by our lives, give testimony to the life and message of Jesus. This is no easy task for young people— or anyone, for that matter. Especially if this is the last time the school will gather, it would provide an opportunity to remind students that their witnessing to the values and lifestyle of Jesus should continue over the summer months as well, even when we are not present to each other as a school community.

The promise that the Spirit will be with us as comfort and strength is a promise that we are not alone in this witnessing. The readings from Acts and Ephesians call attention to the actual event of the Ascension and the kind of witnessing we are called to do. The gospel reading changes with the yearly cycles. To further emphasize the connection between the idea of witnessing and our baptismal call, the rite of sprinkling will replace the penitential rite.

MINISTERS

The students chosen as readers for this liturgy will need to be well rehearsed, especially because of the proper names in the reading from Acts. In the reading from Ephesians, the long sentences will require practice so that the message is clearly communicated. This may be a time to introduce new students to participation in the liturgy, since seniors may have already graduated. Students will be needed to lector, read the intercessions, present gifts, and participate in the entrance procession. If this liturgy is celebrated by the entire community, ushers may also be needed. The presider and homilist will also need to know whether or not this is the last liturgical celebration of the school year.

ENVIRONMENT

Because this solemnity falls in the middle of spring, the use of fresh flowers to bring that atmosphere indoors would enhance the worship space. It would also recall the glory of the Easter season, which is coming to a close. Banners of pastel colors or ribbons would further call attention to the season. A paschal candle should be placed in the altar area (near the ambo would be appropriate today) if at all possible.

MUSIC

This is indeed a time to celebrate. Jesus is risen, alleluia! Let the dancers dance, singers sing, and crashing cymbals be heard! Here is a great opportunity for members of the local band and orchestra program to use their talents in praise. If you have access to handbells, use them throughout the liturgy. They can make hearts sing, even if peer pressure won't let us sing.

"Blessed Be the Lord," although a setting of the Canticle of Zachary, is a great way to begin this celebration: Scripture is fulfilled! Repeat the refrain during the sprinkling rite and go right into the Gloria. Psalm 118 is based on the familiar alleluia response. Use the O FILII ET FILIAE alleluia as the gospel acclamation and even as a response to the prayers of the faithful. During the preparation of the table and gifts and during the recessional, don't hold back on using percussion. Find young people who have "garage bands" who might be surprised you want them for liturgy. The communion song, although somber, helps us focus on our mission to serve, feed, and live the Good News to all people. The repetition in the song makes it a great song for use during Communion, since no worship aid is required. One caution: do watch the tempo. The tendency is to rush this song; keep it slow, but not deadly. (The recording uses a wonderful tempo.)

LITURGY CHECKLIST

- ❏ Copies of readings, given to readers in advance
- ❏ Copy of intercessions, given to intercessor in advance
- ❏ Vestments for presider
- ❏ Lectionary, marked and in place
- ❏ Sacramentary, marked and in place
- ❏ Processional cross in place
- ❏ Candles, in place and lit, including paschal candle (if available)
- ❏ Banners and banner stands in place
- ❏ Bread, wine, water, ciboria and communion cups, coporal, purificator(s), finger bowl, finger towel
- ❏ Bowl of water and aspergill for sprinkling rite
- ❏ Worship aids distributed
- ❏ All involved in the procession are in place—lector, intercessor, banner bearers, any assistants, presider

Other:

ORDER OF WORSHIP

INTRODUCTORY RITES

GATHERING SONG
"Blessed Be the Lord," songs CD/CS-#4, music book #4; *continue through sprinkling rite.*

GREETING

SPRINKLING RITE
Sacramentary, p. 358 (404), C

GLORIA
"Glory to God," basics CD/CS1-#3, music book #16.

OPENING PRAYER
Or: *Sacramentary,*
p. 260 (310), Ascension

Let us pray.

**God of all hope,
today we celebrate the Ascension of Jesus, your Son.
We know that in his leaving
we are left to serve as the witnesses to his life and values.
May your Spirit give us the gift of courage
to be the voice and hands of Jesus in our world.**

**We ask this through our Lord Jesus Christ, your Son,
who lives and reigns with you and the Holy Spirit,
one God, for ever and ever. R/.**

LITURGY OF THE WORD

READING 1
Acts 1:1–11, *Lectionary* #58
Always observe some silence after the reading.

PSALM
"Psalm 118: This Is the Day," basics CD/CS1-#9, music book #22.
Observe some silence after the psalm.

READING 2
Year A, B, C: Ephesians 1:17–23, *Lectionary* #58
Or: Year B: Ephesians 4:1–13 or 1–7, 11–13, *Lectionary* #58
Or: Year C: Hebrews 9:24–28, 10:19–23, *Lectionary* #58
Always observe some silence after the reading.

GOSPEL ACCLAMATION
"Word of Truth and Life," basics CD/CS2-#6, music book #31.
Or: Alleluia refrain based on Psalm 118 above (O FILII ET FILIAE).
You may wish to incense the gospel. See the appendix for suggestions.

GOSPEL   Year A: Matthew 28:16–20, *Lectionary #58*
         Year B: Mark 16:15–20, *Lectionary #58*
         Year C: Luke 24:46–53, *Lectionary #58*

HOMILY/
REFLECTION NOTES

As you prepare the homily for this liturgy, you might want to consider the following. It would also be worth considering if there are neophytes (the newly baptized) in the community to invite one them to share their story within the homily.

What does it mean to be a witness?

What are the things you give witness to? Family? Faith? Education?

How do you give witness to Jesus?

Where do you look for support and strength in giving witness?

What does it mean to be the voice and hands of Jesus today?

GENERAL
INTERCESSIONS

Or: "Prayer of the Faithful," basics CD/CS2-#10, music book #35.

Be sure to add any intentions that are pertinent to your community. The intercessor should be in place before the presider gives the invitation to pray. These prayers may be led from the ambo. Consider random ringing of handbells throughout the intercessions. The assembly's response could be the sung alleluia refrain.

Presider: **Loving God,**
            we come before you with our prayers and needs.
            We trust that you will hear our petitions.

Intercessor: **That those who lead us in faith have the courage to be witnesses to the lifestyle of Jesus, let us pray to the Lord: R/.**

            That all of us who follow Jesus support each other as we share his message, let us pray to the Lord: R/.

            That the presence of the Spirit comfort those separated from the ones they love, let us pray to the Lord: R/.

            Other intentions may be added here.

            For all who have died: that they find lasting peace, let us pray to the Lord: R/.

            The intercessor should face the presider and not leave until the prayer is finished.

Presider: **Loving God,**
            we celebrate the resurrection of Jesus and his return to you in heaven.
            We ask you to hear us and give us courage
            as we keep trying to live out the message of Jesus.

            Grant this in his name. R/.

LITURGY OF THE EUCHARIST

PREPARATION OF THE
ALTAR AND THE GIFTS

"Come, All You People," basics CD/CS2-#1, music book #26.

PRAYER OVER THE GIFTS

Giver of gifts,
take our offerings of bread and wine as a sign of our willingness
to live as followers and friends of your Son, Jesus,
who lives and reigns with you for ever and ever. R/.

EUCHARISTIC PRAYER

Sacramentary, proper preface p. 425 (443), sung preface p. 424 (956);
    p. 542 (502), Eucharistic Prayer I
"Eucharistic Acclamations," basics CD/CS2-#11, music book #36.

COMMUNION RITE

LORD'S PRAYER

SIGN OF PEACE

BREAKING OF THE BREAD

"Lamb of God," basics CD/CS2-#12, music book #37.
Ask the other ministers to help break bread and pour wine so this rite will not be extended.

COMMUNION SONG

"For Living, for Dying," songs CD/CS-#5, music book #5.
Always observe some silence after Communion.

PRAYER AFTER COMMUNION
Or: *Sacramentary*,
p. 261 (311), Ascension

Let us pray.

God,
may our receiving of Jesus in communion
remind us of our closeness to you and each other.
Help us to support each other
as we try to be witnesses to the message of Jesus,
who lives and reigns with you for ever and ever. R/.

CONCLUDING RITE

GREETING AND BLESSING
Or: *Sacramentary*, p. 261
(311), Solemn Blessing

"Blessing," basics CD/CS2-#16, music book #41.

DISMISSAL

RECESSIONAL SONG

"Joyfully Singing," songs CD/CS-#8, music book #8.

PREPARATION FOR ASCENSION EUCHARIST

GIVE THE GIFT OF ASSURANCE

DATE: **TIME:**

LOCATION:

OVERALL THEME   Being witnesses to the message of Jesus.

SCRIPTURE USED   Acts 1:1–11

Year A, B, C: Ephesians 1:17–23 / Or: Year B: Ephesians 4:1–13 or 1–7, 11–13 Or: Year C: Hebrews 9:24–28, 10:19–23

Year A: Matthew 28:16–20 / Year B: Mark 16:15–20 / Year C: Luke 24:46–53

SHORT REFLECTION   It is important to do the necessary catechesis about the events surrounding the Ascension of Jesus. It would be good to reference the symbols of Easter, especially the paschal candle (light), water (new life), oil (strength), the Eucharist (food for the journey). As the school year comes to a close the idea of witnessing to the values and ideals taught during the year takes on a greater significance. After some discussion of what this kind of witnessing means, draw the connection with our call to be Jesus' witnesses. Spend some time exploring what this means in concrete ways. Identify the values and aspects of Jesus message that young people can focus on. Acknowledge with them that it is not always easy to be true to values and beliefs, especially those that may run counter to our culture. Emphasize to them that we are not alone in this challenging work—we are part of a faith community and most importantly, Jesus promises us that he will be with us always, to the end of time.

QUESTIONS FOR STUDENTS TO PONDER
1. What does it mean to be a witness to Jesus' words?
2. How do you witness to the values taught to you by your family?
3. What is the hardest part of the Gospel message for you to live out?
4. What help and support do you need to continue to follow Jesus?

CLOSING COMMENTS   "And know that I am with you always until the end of the world." These words are important to focus on as the Easter season and the academic year come to a close and we are off to summer activities. It is often difficult for young people who struggle with questions of faith to remain consistent in their convictions when not surrounded by a community or group of believers. Since support and community are so integral to the life of an adolescent, centering on Jesus' promise to never leave us alone would be a welcome message and one to leave with them.

Any questions, please contact _____.

EUCHARISTIC BACCALAUREATE

MAY / JUNE

PREPARATION

GETTING STARTED

The baccalaureate liturgy is a significant ritual in Catholic high schools and many parishes. Oftentimes in the past, students graduated—received their diplomas—in the context of the Eucharist. As our understanding of the liturgy evolved and the Mass-graduation combination became very long, high schools adopted the college and university model of separating the baccalaureate liturgy from the graduation ceremony. This liturgy is the one last time that members of the class, their families, friends, and teachers meet together as a faith community in the same space in which they have prayed together for four years. That fact alone endows this event with a great deal of significance. Because every community has its own traditions, mission, and culture, each community will undoubtedly add or subtract elements from this liturgy to reflect what makes them unique. The readings themselves may need to change because of where the celebration falls in the liturgical year. The time of year for this celebration situates it near the solemnities of Ascension and Pentecost. For this reason, in addition to the leave-taking that graduation time marks, the focus is on sending forth, commissioning, building on what has been learned, and taking it into the future. Jesus is leaving his followers, commissioning them, exhorting them to carry on his work and at the same time promising them that they will never be alone. We would hope that our graduates would leave our schools with the values we have shared with them over these four years. To emphasize this sending forth, the entrance procession includes all the graduates in a candle-lighting ceremony. After Communion, the graduates are commissioned by the principal and blessed by their parents. Because of the busyness of this time of year, the procession and commissioning are structured so as not to add any more practices or rehearsals.

It has also become the practice that often home parishes recognize sometime during the period between Ascension and Pentecost those making an education transition. With some minor adaptations, this the liturgy outlined here may be followed.

If the graduation ceremony is to occur at this time, there needs to be some discussion ahead of time regarding when diplomas will be conferred. Some liturgists would wait until after the dismissal, before the final song; others would sing the final song of the liturgy, then confer the diplomas and reprise the final song. This is a local decision to be made together by the presider, rector or pastor, campus minister, and any other competent authority.

Coordinate seating logistics and ritual actions of ministers, graduates, faculty, and parents before hand: e.g., if parents are seated with graduates, they can place their hands on their child's shoulder for the blessing; if they are seated apart from the graduates, consider having parents raise their hands in blessing.

MINISTERS

As much as possible, graduates should fill the roles of lectors, intercessors, presenters of gifts, and eucharistic ministers. Because of the candle procession at the beginning, those who carry in the processional cross, candles, and lectionary should perhaps be representatives of the junior class. The presider of this liturgy should be a priest known to the class or the community in some way. If that is not possible, perhaps someone with a closer connection to the school or the graduating class should offer the reflection. In addition, because there will be a large population of guests, ministers of hospitality, again members of the junior class (or faculty, school board, or parish council), should be on hand to distribute worship aids and direct people to their seats.

ENVIRONMENT

The worship space for this celebration should be enhanced with the appropriate colors of the season as well as reflect colors significant to the school, as long as they do not compete with the liturgical celebration of Easter. This would include any altar or podium antependiums as well as the choice of flowers and plants. Make sure Easter symbols are prominent and not overshadowed by the school symbols, which can have their own prominence at a school's honors night. During the preparation of gifts fill the worship space with candles of all different types. Put them in hurricane lamps and place at varying levels.

MUSIC

Remember: (1) this is a great celebration; (2) there are many guests; (3) there are a myriad of emotions involved; (4) the Church is still in the Easter season; (5) the center of the gathering is not the conferral of diplomas but the celebration of the Eucharist. Therefore: (1) keep things festive; (2) use materials familiar to the whole assembly or which they can easily pick up; (3) be sensitive to the life of this class; (4) enhance the music to the best of the community's abilities; (5) always focus the music on the celebration of the Eucharist (a "pop" song chosen as the "class song" has a more appropriate place at a non-church honors program).

LITURGY CHECKLIST

- ❑ Copies of readings, given to readers in advance
- ❑ Copy of intercessions, given to intercessor in advance
- ❑ Separate podium or lectern (other than the ambo)
- ❑ Tapers or other candles for all graduates and faculty
- ❑ Vestments for presider
- ❑ Lectionary, marked and in place
- ❑ Sacramentary, marked and in place
- ❑ Processional cross in place
- ❑ Candles, in place and lit
- ❑ Banners and banner stands in place
- ❑ Bread, wine, water, ciboria and communion cups, coporal, purificator(s), finger bowl, finger towel
- ❑ Incense pot, incense resins (in incense boat?), charcoal (lit)
- ❑ Worship aids distributed (including blessings)
- ❑ All involved in the procession are in place—lector, intercessor, banner bearers, any assistants, presider

Other:

ORDER OF WORSHIP

INTRODUCTORY RITES

The liturgy begins with the faculty, who enter with lit candles—or someone may carry the paschal candle, from which the faculty members light their candles—and take their places at the front and side aisles. When they are in position, the graduates enter with unlit tapers and light their taper from one of the faculty members and go to their places. The faculty then take their places.

GATHERING SONG   "He Came Down / We Are Marching (Siyahumba)," basics CD/CS1-#2, music book #15.

GREETING   *The celebrant welcomes the graduates, faculty, administration, and the guests.*

We welcome all here.
We gather in the Easter light,
held by the faculty
and passed on to those of you moving on to a new place in life.
Believing that Christ is our light,
we ask for God's light in our lives.

PENITENTIAL RITE
Or: *Sacramentary,* p. 360
(406), invitation B,
form C-ii *(c-2)*

Jesus, during your time on earth
you taught us how to live.
Lord, have mercy. R/.

Jesus, when you left your friends to return to God in heaven,
you commissioned your disciples to carry on your work.
Christ, have mercy. R/.

Jesus, we need your help and the guidance of the Spirit
to live out the message of the Gospel.
Lord, have mercy. R/.

May almighty God have mercy on us,
forgive us our sins,
and bring us to everlasting life. R/.

GLORIA   "Glory to God," basics CD/CS1-#3, music book #16.

OPENING PRAYER
Or: *Sacramentary,*
p. 923 *(834),* #39-B,
In Thanksgiving

Let us pray.

Loving God,
who has seen us through days of learning and growth,
we know that you love each of us and want our happiness.

Help us not to lose sight of all that we have learned.
Stay with each of us as we continue into the future
and remind us of the rich heritage that is ours
as members of this faith community.

We ask this through our Lord Jesus Christ, your Son,
who lives and reigns with you and the Holy Spirit,
one God, for ever and ever. R/.

The presider indicates that all may extinguish their candles.

LITURGY OF THE WORD

READING 1

Philippians 4:4–9, *Lectionary #740-10*
Always observe some silence after the reading.

PSALM

"Psalm 118: This Is the Day," basics CD/CS1-#9, music book #22.
Observe some silence after the psalm.

GOSPEL ACCLAMATION

Alleluia, using melody from "Psalm 118" above (O FILII ET FILIAE).
Or: "Word of Truth and Life," basics CD/CS2-#6, music book #31.
You may wish to incense the gospel. See the appendix for suggestions.

GOSPEL

John 14:1–6, *Lectionary #283*

HOMILY/ REFLECTION NOTES

As you prepare your reflection, you may want to consider these questions.
What are your memories or reflections on your leave-taking from high school?
What values or messages that you received at that time have stayed with you?
What significance do Jesus' words about being the way, the truth,
    and life have for you at this juncture? As you were leaving high school?
Where were the most powerful lessons you were taught? By whom?
What important message would you like to share with these young men
    and women?

GENERAL INTERCESSIONS

Or: "Prayer of the Faithful," basics CD/CS2-#10, music book #35.
Or: "Penitential Litany (Kyrie)," basics CD/CS2-#7, music book #32.
*Be sure to add any intentions that are pertinent to your community. The intercessor
should be in place before the presider gives the invitation to pray. These prayers may
be led from the ambo.*

Presider:

**God, our loving parent,
who gives us comfort and hope in our beginnings and endings,
we come to you, trusting that in your love you will hear our prayers.**

Intercessor:

**For our Church, who calls us to be of service, let us pray to the
Lord: R/.**

For a world seeking leaders of peace and justice, let us pray to the Lord: R/.

For the administration, faculty, and staff of this school, who have taken part in our growth during these four years, let us pray to the Lord: R/.

For our parents, whose support in so many ways has been there for us unconditionally: that they be blessed with peace, let us pray to the Lord: R/.

For our friends, who have shared with us all the laughter, tears, late nights, and early mornings: that they may know how much we love and cherish them, let us pray to the Lord: R/.

For the class of ____: that God will guide each of us into our futures to seek the way, the truth, and the life, let us pray to the Lord: R/.

For all those who have gone before us to be in God's presence forever, let us pray to the Lord: R/.

The intercessor should face the presider and not leave until the prayer is finished.

Presider: **God,**
we know that we have so much to be thankful for
as we look back and look ahead.
We ask you to remain with each one of us
as we continue on this journey. R/.

LITURGY OF THE EUCHARIST

PREPARATION OF THE ALTAR AND THE GIFTS

"Send Down the Fire," basics CD/CS2-#2, music book #27.

PRAYER OVER THE GIFTS
Or: *Sacramentary,*
p. 923 (834), #39-B,
In Thanksgiving

Loving God,
accept these gifts from us who celebrate this time of ending
    and beginning.
May we always recognize our union with each other and you in
    the Eucharist.

We ask this through Christ our Lord. R/.

EUCHARISTIC PRAYER

Sacramentary, p. 548 (509), Eucharistic Prayer II
"Eucharistic Acclamations," basics CD/CS2-#11, music book #36.

COMMUNION RITE

LORD'S PRAYER

SIGN OF PEACE

BREAKING OF THE BREAD
"Lamb of God," basics CD/CS2-#12, music book #37.
Ask the other ministers to help break bread and pour wine so this rite will not be extended.

COMMUNION SONG
"Psalm 34: Taste and See," basics CD/CS1-#7, music book #20.
Always observe some silence after Communion.

RITUAL
After Communion, the principal comes to the podium and shares some personal words to the graduates and ends them with words of sending forth in the spirit of the Gospel and the school's mission. She or he invites the graduates to stand and respond together:

Graduates: **Nurtured by the love of our parents, inspired by the guidance of our teachers, and bound by the precious gifts of friendship, we have been blessed. This enables us to welcome tomorrow with hope, with confidence, and with the belief that we can make a difference. We, the graduating Class of _____, receive this commission and accept the challenge to shape the future.**

Presider: **Parents, please stand,
place your hand on your graduate's shoulder,
and answer "Amen" to each portion of the blessing.**

**Bless our daughters and sons, Lord,
as we stand proudly in the light of their achievements.
We pray that they may continue to grow in mind and heart,
in wisdom and compassion,
in faith and gentleness. R/.**

**Lord, help our graduating daughters and sons to realize the
 deep pride we feel
as we celebrate their accomplishments today.**

**Enable these graduates to see clearly
that they can choose a meaningful life,
that they must dare to dream,
and above all,
that they are dearly loved. R/.**

And may they be blessed, Father, Son, ✠ and Holy Spirit. R/.

Choir or cantor may sing "Blessing," basics CD/CS2-#16, music book #41.

PRAYER AFTER COMMUNION
Or: *Sacramentary*,
p. 923 *(834)*, #39-B,
In Thanksgiving

Let us pray.

Almighty God,
may this Eucharist we have shared
remind us of the faith and community that draws us all together as
your children of one family
no matter where the future may take us.

Grant this through Christ our Lord. R/.

CONCLUDING RITE

GREETING AND BLESSING

Book of Blessings, p. 94–95, #192–194 as appropriate.
Or: "Blessing," basics CD/CS2-#16, music book #41, *if not sung above.*

DISMISSAL

RECESSIONAL SONG

"Now," songs CD/CS-#13, music book #13.

PREPARATION FOR BACCALAUREATE EUCHARIST

GIVE THE GIFT OF EXPERIENCE

DATE: **TIME:**

LOCATION:

OVERALL THEME   Graduation, witness, and moving on.

SCRIPTURE USED   Philippians 4:4–9 / John 14:1–6

SHORT REFLECTION   As we go forth, it would be a wonderful time to reflect on high school life. What have you learned? What will you take with you? Take time to have students look to the future and see how the past years have formed who and what they are. Connect this to the Easter season (a time of rebirth) or even the Emmaus story (recognition of Jesus and the "burning" hearts of the apostles).

QUESTIONS FOR   1. When you entered high school, what were your thoughts and expectations?
STUDENTS TO PONDER   2. Reflect on a time Jesus helped you in your way as a student.
   3. What have your high school years taught you about begin God's witness to the world?

CLOSING COMMENTS   Although these students move on, their stories are a part of our community. Affirm their "light" to the community and challenge them to go after ideas that are grounded in the justice and values of Christ's teachings.

Any questions, please contact _____.

EUCHARISTIC CELEBRATION OF THE END OF THE SCHOOL YEAR

MAY / JUNE

PREPARATION

GETTING STARTED

Just as the school year begins by gathering the entire community together, it is appropriate to bring closure to the year by once again sharing the Eucharist as a school. This may be a little more difficult to pull off primarily because of final exams and the seniors having already graduated in some instances. But as a faith community that has prayed together and marked most significant events by gathering to worship, it is important to work through some of the scheduling obstacles to make this happen. Not only does it bring closure to the school year, it marks the leave-taking that happens every May or June. Many students may not be returning for a variety of reasons; staff members may be seeking employment elsewhere; and inevitably, events over the summer break may bring about unexpected departures from both students and teachers. So, we gather the community together for one last time to mark the leave-taking, to note the passages, and to pray that we continue to walk with God during the long break. The Scripture chosen for this liturgy highlights the idea of being or going on a journey. The first reading from Corinthians talks about walking by faith and maintaining that faith whether near or far away. The gospel is the Emmaus story, reminding us to keep our eyes and ears open so we may recognize the presence of Jesus no matter where we are.

As for the passages, if seniors have already graduated, the torch has been passed and the juniors already see themselves as the senior members of the community. Sophomores look forward to being juniors, and freshmen are just happy to have completed their first year and look forward to returning to something familiar. The optional blessing at the end connects the passages with the leave-taking.

MINISTERS

Because of everything else going on at the end of the year, those selected for the various roles in the liturgy should already have some familiarity with them. A lector and a reader for intercessions are needed in addition to those who carry the processional cross and candles.

ENVIRONMENT

School colors and banners used at the opening school liturgy could be used as the year is brought to a close. A table or stand for the symbols or additional candles needs to be in place. For the closing blessing, a bowl of water and aspergill are needed. Blessing with water will formalize the dismissal and leave-taking. Consider using candles to represent each class; they could be of different color and held by representatives. You may want to set up a three-dimensional collage of the past year away from the altar.

MUSIC

Since the seniors will not likely be present, this would be a good time to recognize up-and-coming talents. Prepare yourself as a music minister starting all over again. That's OK—our work in ministry never ends. Besides, you've been preparing the younger ensemble members all along, right?

During the last song, have percussionists help move the assembly from the worship space and celebrate into the world!

LITURGY CHECKLIST

- ❑ Copies of readings, given to readers in advance
- ❑ Copy of intercessions, given to intercessor in advance
- ❑ Vestments for presider
- ❑ Lectionary, marked and in place
- ❑ Sacramentary, marked and in place
- ❑ Processional cross in place
- ❑ Candles, in place and lit
- ❑ Banners and banner stands in place
- ❑ Any additional candles or symbols
- ❑ Bread, wine, water, ciboria and communion cups, coporal, purificator(s), finger bowl, finger towel
- ❑ Incense pot, incense resins (in incense boat?), charcoal (lit)
- ❑ Bowl of water and aspergill
- ❑ Worship aids distributed
- ❑ All involved in the procession are in place—lector, intercessor, banner bearers, any assistants, presider

Other:

ORDER OF WORSHIP

INTRODUCTORY RITES

GATHERING SONG   "Holy Ground," songs CD/CS-#2, music book #2.

GREETING: We gather in this space with the future sophomores, juniors and
seniors of _____ High School.
We thank God for the gifts of this year
and ask him to walk with us as we separate from each other
for the summer.

PENITENTIAL RITE   My friends,
let us look back on this year
and think about those times we have hurt our friends,
or let people down.

I confess to almighty God . . .

May almighty God have mercy on us . . .

OPENING PRAYER
Or: *Sacramentary*,
p. 888 (805), #12,
For the Laity

Let us pray.

Loving God,
we come together for the last time this school year.
We bring with us all of our memories of good times and sad times;
the fun and the work times that we shared.
We ask you to bless the summer days ahead with peace and safety
as we leave this place.
Help us to continue to walk with you
even when we are apart from each other.

We ask you this through our Lord Jesus Christ, your Son,
who lives and reigns with you and the Holy Spirit,
one God, for ever and ever. R/.

LITURGY OF THE WORD

READING 1   2 Corinthians 5:6–10, *Lectionary #93*
Always observe some silence after the reading.

PSALM   "Psalm 104: Lord, Send Out Your Spirit," basics CD/CS1-#11, music book #24.
Observe some silence after the psalm.

GOSPEL ACCLAMATION	"Word of Truth and Life," basics CD/CS2-#6, music book #31. *You may wish to incense the gospel. See the appendix for suggestions.*
GOSPEL	Luke 24:13–35, *Lectionary #263*
HOMILY/ REFLECTION NOTES	*You may want to consider the following questions as you prepare your homily.* When you were in school, what did summer vacation mean to you? What was difficult about making the transition from school into summer time? Think about the disciples in the gospel reading meeting a stranger. What would you tell a stranger about this past year? What actions this past year reminds you of Gospel values? What will be different for you this summer than last, and how can Christ's presence be part of that?
GENERAL INTERCESSIONS	Or: "Prayer of the Faithful," basics CD/CS2-#10, music book #35. *Be sure to add any intentions that are pertinent to your community. The intercessor should be in place before the presider gives the invitation to pray. These prayers may be led from the ambo.*

Presider: **We bring together our prayers and needs as a school community for the last time this year. As always, we are confident that God hears us.**

Intercessor: **For teachers and administrators who have walked with us this year: may the days of summer bring them peace and relaxation, let us pray to the Lord: R/.**

For our parents and families, whose support this year made the journey so much easier: that they know how grateful we are for their presence in our lives, let us pray to the Lord: R/.

For our friends: that they may have a safe and healthy summer and that we will join them again in the new school year, let us pray to the Lord: R/.

For all of us: that God's blessing go with us as we leave for the summer, let us pray to the Lord: R/.

Other intentions may be added here.

For those among our families and friends who have died this year: that they may enjoy God's everlasting presence: let us pray to the Lord: R/.

The intercessor should face the presider and not leave until the prayer is finished.

Presider: **Almighty God,**
we believe that you are always present with us.
Stay near to us and the people we love in the days that we are
apart from one another.
We ask this in the name of Jesus. R/.

LITURGY OF THE EUCHARIST

PREPARATION OF THE
ALTAR AND THE GIFTS

"With the Lord," songs CD/CS-#7, music book #7.

PRAYER OVER
THE GIFTS
Or: *Sacramentary,*
p. 888 (805), #12,
For the Laity

Timeless God,
you know us so well,
better than we know ourselves.
Take these gifts of bread and wine
and bless us with what we need to be faithful to you over the
summer ahead.

Grant this through Christ our Lord. R/.

EUCHARISTIC PRAYER

Eucharist Prayer for Various Needs II, or *Sacramentary,* p. 548 (509),
Eucharistic Prayer II
"Eucharistic Acclamations," basics CD/CS2-#11, music book #36.

COMMUNION RITE

LORD'S PRAYER

SIGN OF PEACE

BREAKING OF
THE BREAD

"Lamb of God," basics CD/CS2-#12, music book #37.
Ask the other ministers to help break bread and pour wine so this rite will not be
extended.

COMMUNION SONG

"Psalm 23: Shepherd Me, O God," basics CD/CS1-#10, music book #23.
Always observe some silence after Communion.

PRAYER AFTER
COMMUNION
Or: *Sacramentary,*
p. 888 (805), #12,
For the Laity

Let us pray.

Loving God,
having shared Communion with one another often in this past year,
we ask that this blessing of shared faith support us in the days ahead
until we return as a community

to once again celebrate in your presence and the presence of Jesus, who lives and reigns with you for ever and ever. R/.

CONCLUDING RITE

GREETING AND BLESSING

Or: "Blessing," basics CD/CS2-#16, music book #41.
Or: *Sacramentary*, 575 (533), #14, Ordinary Time V

The presider asks each group in turn to stand and addresses them with the following words. As he prays the blessing, he sprinkles them with water.

Freshmen
You leave behind the feelings of uncertainty and fear of the unknown
    with which you began the year in a new school.
You look toward your return with your new friends to welcome
    the first year students.
May God watch over you and bless you in the summer
until you return safely in the fall.

Sophomores
You leave behind the struggles of being right in the middle
as well as the challenges of driver's ed.
You look forward to returning as upperclassmen and -women at last,
secure in the relationships that helped you through this year.
May God watch over you and bless you in the summer
until you return safely in the fall.

Juniors
You leave behind those initial challenges of balancing difficult
    courses and a part-time job
as well as all those other demands on your time.
You look forward to making your last year full of special memories.
May God watch over you and bless you in the summer
until you return safely in the fall.

Teachers, Administrators, and Staff
You leave behind all the difficulties and successes of the year.
You look forward to starting next year with new energy and
    new ideas.
May God watch over you and bless you in the summer until you
    return safely in the fall.

May almighty God bless all of you,
the Father, and the Son, ✠ and the Holy Spirit. R/.

DISMISSAL

RECESSIONAL SONG

"We Are Marching (Siyahumba)," basics CD/CS1-#2, music book #15.

PREPARATION FOR THE EUCHARISTIC CELEBRATION OF THE END OF SCHOOL YEAR

GIVE THE GIFT OF A PERSEVERANCE

DATE: **TIME:**

LOCATION:

OVERALL THEME   Reflection on the past year, transition to the next.

SCRIPTURE USED   2 Corinthians 5:6–10 / Luke 24:13–35

SHORT REFLECTION   It is certainly difficult to focus seriously on any issues as the summer vacation becomes more proximate; however, assuming that there is some time for reflection and preparation prior to this liturgy, students might be asked to think about the gifts, challenges, and learning that they experienced during the year. This could take the form of a journaling activity or a simple listing. Any opportunity for young people to take their leave of the school year in the context of thoughtfulness and prayer might encourage a heightened level of awareness regarding the many chances for growth they experienced in the past ten months. Some encouragement to recognize Christ's presence in these gifted moments would set the stage for being able to recognize his presence in future events.

QUESTIONS FOR STUDENTS TO PONDER   1. What sensory things do you remember of the past year's liturgies?

You might provide some aid by quietly recalling the various liturgical gatherings by name or writing them on the chalkboard, such as:

New school year; morning prayer; class unity (ring ceremony, retreat); commissioning of student leaders; community service; team or ensemble prayers; All Saints; All Souls (or memorial service); Thanksgiving; Advent reconciliation; Immaculate Conception (or other Marian celebration); blessing of the new year; Martin Luther King Day; Ash Wednesday; Lent reconciliation; Ascension

2. In what ways were you able to recognize Christ's presence in the experiences of this past school year?
3. What challenges do you face in living out gospel values in the coming weeks of summer?

CLOSING COMMENTS   The leave-taking at the end of a school year finds everyone breathing a long-held sigh of relief. We let go of the work and structure that was shared for ten months and embrace the prospect of rest and relaxation. In that context, we pray in thanksgiving for the gifts of the school year as well as for everyone's safe return in the fall.

Any questions, please contact _____.

APPENDIX

COMMUNION
BREAD RECIPE

2/3 cup unbleached white flour

1/3 cup whole wheat flour

1/2 cup sparkling water (such as Perrier)

1. Preheat the oven to 400 degrees. Spray a 9″ pie plate with cooking spray (Pam) and wipe out the excess.

2. Mix the ingredients in a cold bowl. Add more water if necessary to form a ball. Flatten the dough into the pie plate and score into 100 pieces.

3. Bake bread for 15 minutes. Prick the top with a fork, turn loaf over, and bake five more minutes. Turn over again and bake five more minutes.

4. Cool on a wire rack. Wrap tightly and store in a plastic bag. The bread is best used as soon as possible, but it can be frozen for later use.

BANNERS

There are simple ways to make banners so they do not take an inordinate amount of time and energy. The banner poles may be made of PVC pipe (available in hardware stores and building centers in the plumbing area), which is light and can be easily cut to different lengths. The stands can be simply made of a square of wood to which a length of metal pipe can be attached. The PVC poles should fit inside or slip over the outside of the metal pipe of the stand. You might need to speak to the engineer or maintenance person about what you need.

The PVC pipe is perfect for ribbon banners. There are many two-way and four-way connectors which can make "arms" from which the ribbons can hang. The ribbons might have bells attached to them. A similar, but more sophisticated look can be achieved with lengths of cloth that have been hemmed. The "arms" of the banner pole can be cut to any width. There are even small caps for a more finished look to the end of the pipe. The pipe is flexible, so it cannot be cut too long or support too much weight without bending.

Larger banners may be hung on a dowel rod to which wire or string is attached. This can be hung on an "S" hook, which can be hung on the pole. These tend to slide around and may need to be anchored by taping the hook to the pole. Larger pieces of cloth look good festooned with ribbons. Don't worry about visuals on the banners. They do not have to do any more than add color, movement, and height to a procession.

Another good shape is the pennant. Have someone make a few in various colors with a pocket that can slip directly over the banner pole. They hang nicely in a procession, but tend to "shrivel" when set into a stand. They might be retired to the sacristy until the end of Mass.

INCENSE

A good encyclopedia article will give you information about incense and a Catholic encyclopedia will give you a history of its use in our tradition. The *General Introduction to the Roman Missal* suggests "The use of incense is optional...during the entrance procession...at the beginning of Mass, to incense the altar...at the...proclamation of the gospel...preparation of the gifts, to incense them...the altar, priest, and people...at the showing of the...bread and chalice after consecration." (#235) Incense delights the nose the way color delights the eye. While a few people are sensitive to incense, the majority will enjoy it, especially the youth, if they are given a chance to talk about it.

Most young people will love to be asked to carry the parish censer (thurible) or an incense pot. Good, inexpensive clay pots may be often found at local plant nurseries and craft stores. Be sure the pot has no hole in the bottom and color is fired on. The pot should be deep enough to hold a good deal of sand or gravel to insulate the carrier from the heat of the burning charcoal. Always test the pot by burning a charcoal or two in it before using it in Eucharist. See how well the sand insulates the sides and bottom of the pot and how hot they eventually get. The insulation is especially important if the pot is to be carried.

Use a pair of tongs to hold the charcoal when preparing the censer. The charcoal often sparks, so be careful of clothes and rug. Light the charcoal about ten minutes before the gathering procession begins. When it is gray it is ready to burn incense. A parish often keeps a supply of incense resins in a dish called the incense boat. The assisting ministers should know all about this and should know when to refresh the charcoal if incense is used at the gospel and the preparation of the gifts.

THE LITURGICAL CALENDAR

The liturgical calendar is the listing of the solemnities, feasts, memorials, and seasons that Catholics celebrate. The calendar is published in many forms. The document *General Norms for the Liturgical Year and the Calendar* may be found in the Sacramentary.

GLOSSARY

ALB	A long, white garment worn by priests, deacons, servers, and other ministers at liturgy.
ALMS	Money set aside to share with the poor.
AMBO	The pulpit, which is the appropriate place from which Scripture (including the psalm) is proclaimed, the homily is shared, and the intercessions are led.
ASPERGILL	The perforated ball with a handle used to sprinkle water.
ASSEMBLY	The group of people who have gathered for community worship.
ASSISTANT	A person who is in attendance to the presider.
BOBECHE	The paper "collar" that catches drips from congregational candles.
CANTOR	The minister who leads the sung prayer and proclaims the psalm.
CHALICE	The cup used at the altar that holds the consecrated wine.
CHASUBLE	The vestment worn over the alb by the priest at Eucharist.
CIBORIUM	The dish or covered vessel used by the minister of communion.
CINCTURE	A rope-like belt used by the priest and altar servers.
COMMUNION CUPS	Additional chalices used to distribute the consecrated wine at Communion.
CONGREGATIONAL CANDLE	The thin candles (tapers) used at the Easter Vigil and other light services.
CORPORAL	A square, white piece of cloth on the altar on which the bread and wine are set.
CREDENCE TABLE	A small table near the altar that holds the chalice and paten, water for washing of hands, holy water bucket, etc.
DALMATIC	The vestment worn over the alb by the deacon at Eucharist.
INCENSE BOAT	The small covered dish with a spoon that holds a supply of incense resins.
INCENSE POT	The pot or bowl in which incense resins may be burned with charcoal.

INTERCESSOR	One who leads the general intercessions; on Sunday it may be the deacon.
LECTIONARY	The large book, often with a red cover, which holds the readings for every day of the week; some parishes have a separate Book of the Gospels.
LECTOR	One who proclaims the Scripture.
PASCHAL CANDLE	The tall, special candle blessed at the Easter Vigil. It is placed in the altar area and lit during the fifty days of Easter. It would also be appropriate at funerals and other memorial services.
PERICOPE	A section of Scripture chosen from the Bible for proclamation at liturgy.
PRESIDER	Usually refers to the priest (celebrant) of the Mass.
PROCESSIONAL CROSS	A cross mounted on a pole used to lead processions.
PROCESSOR	One who carries something in a procession.
PURIFICATOR	A small square of white cloth used by the presider and communion minister to wipe the chalice or communion cup.
SACRAMENTARY	The large, often red, book used at the presider chair and the altar containing the prayers for each Mass.
STOLE	The long, thin garment worn by the ordained when they exercise their offices. The priest wears it around the neck and the deacon wears it over the shoulder.
WORSHIP AID (OR PARTICIPATION AID)	A booklet or paper containing music or prayers the assembly uses to pray. (The school or parish needs to get permission from the publisher to print music even if it comes from the parish hymnals.)
WORSHIP SPACE	The place where the Church meets to pray.

Bibliography

Book of Blessings (The Roman Ritual). New York: Catholic Book Publishing, 1989.

Catechism of the Catholic Church. English translation. Washington, D.C.: United States Catholic Conference, Inc., 1994.

Catholic Household Blessings and Prayers. Washington, D.C.: United States Catholic Conference, Inc., 1988.

Connel, Martin, ed. *The Catholic Documents: A Parish Resource*. Chicago: Liturgy Training Publications, 1996.

Fleming, Austin. *Preparing for Liturgy*. Chicago: Liturgy Training Publications, 1997.

From Age to Age: The Challenge of Worship with Adolescents. Washington, D.C.: National Federation for Catholic Youth Ministry, Inc., 1997.

Hoffman, Elizabeth. *The Liturgy Documents: A Parish Resource*. 3rd edition. Chicago: Liturgy Training Publications, 1991.

Lectionary for Mass. New York: Catholic Book Publishing Company, 1974. Also published by Liturgical Press (Collegeville, Minn.).

Melloh, John Allyn, SM and William G. Storey, eds. *Praise God in Song: Ecumenical Daily Prayer*. Chicago: GIA Publications, Inc., 1979.

The Sacramentary. New York: Catholic Book Publishing Company, 1985. Also published by Liturgical Press (Collegeville, Minn.).

Tufano, Victoria, ed. *Sourcebook for Sundays and Seasons*. Annual. Chicago: Liturgy Training Publications.

Williams, Vivian E. *Classroom Prayer Basics*. Laurel, Md.: The Pastoral Press, 1997.

About the Authors

LINDA M. BALTIKAS

Linda Baltikas is a religious education instructor and Curriculum Coordinator at Queen of Peace High School in Burbank, Illinois. She has been involved in education in the Archdiocese of Chicago for twenty-eight years at the elementary and secondary levels. Eight years of parish and elementary school ministry have included school religion program and liturgy coordination, work with sacramental programs, and religious education for teens through adults. In addition to classroom teaching at the secondary level, she has served as campus minister, coordinating liturgies and retreats, for fourteen years. She is a graduate of Loyola University, Institute of Pastoral Studies, in Chicago, Illinois, and is completing the program in Educational Administration at Dominican University in River Forest, Illinois.

ROBERT W. PIERCY

Robert W. Piercy, Jr., is a liturgist, musician, and national speaker. He lives in Chicago, Illinois, and serves as catechetical consultant for GIA Publications, Inc. Ecumenically, he serves as the Catholic Consultant for the American Bible Society and also works with Loyola Press. His most recent books are *When Children Gather*, eucharistic and non-eucharistic prayer services for children; *Walking by Faith*, prayer services for religious education programs; *Give Your Gifts*, prayer services for teens; and *Celebrating Our Faith*, prayer services in preparation for the sacraments of initiation. Piercy has a recurring column in the GIA *Quarterly* on liturgy and catechesis.

JEAN E. BROSS-JUDGE

Jean E. Bross-Judge has served as Prayer and Worship Coordinator for the National Catholic Youth Convention (1997 and 1999) and the National Conference on Catholic Youth Ministry (1998), both sponsored by the National Federation for Catholic Youth Ministry. She is the Assistant Director of Youth Programming for the American Bible Society and is a former Associate Director of Youth Ministry, Archdiocese of Cincinnati. Ms. Bross-Judge is a sought-after national keynote and workshop presenter for youth and adult audiences, who explores the topics of liturgy, prayer, spirituality, Scripture, and adolescence.

144